ᴄᴠ *New British Poetry*

New British Poetry

EDITED BY

Don Paterson

AND

Charles Simic

Graywolf Press
SAINT PAUL, MINNESOTA

Publication of this volume is made possible in part by a grant provided by the
Minnesota State Arts Board, through an appropriation by the Minnesota State
Legislature; a grant from the Wells Fargo Foundation Minnesota; and a grant from
the National Endowment for the Arts. Significant support has also been provided
by the Bush Foundation; Target, Marshall Field's and Mervyn's with support from
the Target Foundation; the McKnight Foundation; and other generous contribu-
tions from foundations, corporations, and individuals. To these organizations and
individuals we offer our heartfelt thanks.

MINNESOTA
STATE ARTS BOARD

NATIONAL
ENDOWMENT
FOR THE ARTS

Published by Graywolf Press
2402 University Avenue, Suite 203
Saint Paul, Minnesota 55114
All rights reserved.

www.graywolfpress.org

Published in the United States of America
Printed in Canada

ISBN 1-55597-394-9

2 4 6 8 9 7 5 3 1
First Graywolf Printing, 2004

Library of Congress Control Number: 2003111080

Cover design: Christa Schoenbrodt, Studio Haus

Acknowledgments

Allnutt, Gillian. "Scheherazade," "The Silk Light of Advent," "Held To," and "The Road Home" from *Lintel* by Gillian Allnutt, published by Bloodaxe Books, 2001. "Notes on living inside the lightbulb" from *Nantucket and the Angel* by Gillian Allnutt, published by Bloodaxe Books, 1997. Reprinted by permission of Bloodaxe Books.

Armitage, Simon. "Poem" from *Kid* by Simon Armitage, published by Faber & Faber Ltd. "The Tyre" from *CloudCuckooLand* by Simon Armitage, published by Faber & Faber Ltd. "The Dead Sea Poems" from *The Dead Sea Poems* by Simon Armitage, published by Faber & Faber Ltd. Reprinted by permission of Faber & Faber Ltd. "Very Simply Topping Up the Brake Fluid" from *Zoom!* by Simon Armitage, published by Bloodaxe Books, 1995. Reprinted by permission of Bloodaxe Books.

Ash, John. "The Ungrateful Citizens," "The Sky My Husband," and "Memories of Italy" from *Selected Poems* by John Ash, published by Carcanet Press Limited, 1996. Reprinted by permission of Carcanet Press Limited.

Bhatt, Sujata. " શેરડી (Shérdi)," "Muliebrity," and "What Is Worth Knowing?" from *Brunizem* by Sujata Bhatt, published by Carcanet Press Limited, 1998. "Fischerhude, 2001" from *A Colour for Solitude* by Sujata Bhatt, published by Carcanet Press Limited, 2002. Reprinted by permission of Carcanet Press Limited.

Burnside, John. "Parousia" and "The Old Gods" from *Swimming in the Flood* by John Burnside, published by Jonathan Cape, 1999. Reprinted by permission of The Random House Group Ltd.

Crawford, Robert. "The Saltcoats Structuralists" and "Alba Einstein" from *A Scottish Assembly* by Robert Crawford, published by Chatto & Windus, 1990. "Fiat Lux" from *The Tip of My Tongue* by Robert Crawford, published by Jonathan Cape, 2003. "The Result" from *Spirit Machines* by Robert Crawford, published by Jonathan Cape, 1999. "The Handshakes" from *Masculinity* by Robert Crawford, published by Jonathan Cape, 1996. Reprinted by permission of The Random House Group Ltd.

D'Aguiar, Fred. "Airy Hall Nightmare" and "The Cow *Perseverance*" from *Airy Hall* by Fred D'Aguiar, published by Chatto & Windus, 1989. Reprinted by permission of The Random House Group, Ltd. "Sound Bite" and "Home" from *British Subjects* by Fred D'Aguiar, published by Bloodaxe Books, 1993. Reprinted by permission of Bloodaxe Books.

Didsbury, Peter. "The Shorter Life," "That Old-Time Religion," "Part of the Bridge," and "Chandlery" from *Scenes from a Long Sleep: New & Collected Poems* by Peter Didsbury, published by Bloodaxe Books, 2003. Reprinted by permission of Bloodaxe Books.

Donaghy, Michael. "Machines," "Shibboleth," and "The Bacchae" from *Shibboleth* by Michael Donaghy, published by Picador Press, 1988. "Caliban's Books" and "A Repertoire" from *Conjure* by Michael Donaghy, published by Picador Press, 2000. Reprinted by permission of Macmillan, London, UK.

Duffy, Carol Ann. "Prayer" from *Mean Time* by Carol Ann Duffy, published by Anvil Press Poetry, 1993, and "Warming Her Pearls" from *Selling Manhattan* by Carol Ann Duffy, published by Anvil Press Poetry, 1987. Reprinted by permission of Anvil Press Poetry. "Circe" and "Little Red-Cap" from *The World's Wife* by Carol Ann Duffy, published by Faber & Faber Ltd., 1999. Reprinted by permission of Faber & Faber Ltd.

Duhig, Ian. "Fundamentals" from *The Bradford Count* by Ian Duhig, published by Bloodaxe Books, 1991. Reprinted by permission of Ian Duhig. "Chocolate Soldier" from *Nominies* by Ian Duhig, published by Bloodaxe Books, 1998. Reprinted by permission of Ian Duhig. "The Lammas Hireling" from *The Lammas Hireling* by Ian Duhig, published by Picador Press. Reprinted by permission of Macmillan, London, UK.

Farley, Paul. "Treacle" and "The Lamp" from *The Boy from the Chemist Is Here to See You* by Paul Farley, published by Picador Press, 1998. "Diary Moon," "An Interior," and "Peter and the Dyke" from *The Ice Age*, by Paul Farley, published by Picador Press, 2002. Reprinted by permission of Macmillan, London, UK.

Fenton, James. "Wind," "In a Notebook," and "A Staffordshire Murderer" from *The Memory of War/ Children in Exile: Poems 1968–1983*, published by Penguin Press, 1992. Reprinted by permission of Peters Fraser & Dunlop on behalf of James Fenton.

Ford, Mark. "Looping the Loop," "The Long Man," and "Early to Bed, Early to Rise" from *Soft Sift* by Mark Ford, published by Faber & Faber Ltd., 2001. Reprinted by permission of Faber & Faber Ltd.

Glenday, John. "Concerning the Atoms of the Soul," "A Day at the Seaside," and "The Empire of Lights" from *Undark* © John Glenday, published by Peterloo Poets, 1995, reproduced by permission of Peterloo Poets. "The Garden" and "Hydrodamalis Gigas" reprinted by permission of John Glenday.

Greenlaw, Lavinia. "Reading Akhmatova in Midwinter" and "Three" from *A World Where News Travelled Slowly* by Lavinia Greenlaw, published by Faber & Faber Ltd., 1997. "The Spirit of the Staircase" and "Zombies" from *Minsk* by Lavinia Greenlaw, published by Faber & Faber Ltd., 2003. "Electricity" from *Night Photograph* by Lavinia Greenlaw, published by Faber & Faber Ltd., 1993. Reprinted by permission of Faber & Faber Ltd.

Herbert, W. N. "Slow Animals Crossing" from *The Big Bumper Book of Troy* by W. N. Herbert, published by Bloodaxe Books, 2002. "Cabaret McGonagall," "Smirr," and "The King and Queen of Dumfriesshire" from *Cabaret McGonagall* by W. N. Herbert, published by Bloodaxe Books, 1996. Reprinted by permission of Bloodaxe Books.

Hill, Selima. "I Will Be Arriving Next Thursday in My Wedding-Dress," "I Know I Ought to Love You," "My Sister's Jeans," and "Please Can I Have a Man" from *Violet* by Selima Hill, published by Bloodaxe Books, 1997. "A Small Hotel" from *A Little Book of Meat* by Selima Hill, published by Bloodaxe Books, 1993. Reprinted by permission of Bloodaxe Books.

Hofmann, Michael. "Ancient Evenings, " "The Late Richard Dadd, 1817–1886," and "The Machine That Cried" from *Acrimony* by Michael Hofmann, published by Faber & Faber Ltd., 1986. "Lament for Crassus" from *Corona, Corona* by Michael Hofmann, published by Faber & Faber Ltd., 1993. Reprinted by permission of Faber & Faber Ltd.

Jamie, Kathleen. "The Bogey-Wife" from *Jizzen* by Kathleen Jamie, published by Picador Press, 1999. Reprinted by permission of Macmillan, London, UK. "The Way We Live" and "Skeins o Geese" from *Mr & Mrs Scotland Are Dead: Poems 1980–1994* by Kathleen Jamie, published by Bloodaxe Books, 2002. Reprinted by permission of Bloodaxe Books. "Pipistrelles" and "The Hill-track" reprinted by permission of Kathleen Jamie.

Jenkins, Alan. "Visiting" and "Portrait of a Lady" from *Harm* by Alan Jenkins, published by Chatto & Windus, 1994. "Barcelona" and "Inheritance" from *The Drift* by Alan Jenkins, published by Chatto & Windus, 2000. Reprinted by permission of The Random House Group Ltd.

Kay, Jackie. "Even the Trees," "In my country," "Finger," and excerpt from "Other Lovers" from *Other Lovers* by Jackie Kay, published by Bloodaxe Books, 1993. "The Shoes of Dead Comrades" from *Off Colour* by Jackie Kay, published by Bloodaxe Books, 1998. Reprinted by permission of Bloodaxe Books.

Lewis, Gwyneth. "Pentecost" and excerpt from "Welsh Espionage: ix Advice on Adultery" from *Parables & Faxes* by Gwyneth Lewis, published by Bloodaxe Books, 1995. "'One day, feeling hungry'," "Woods," and "The Flaggy Shore" from *Zero Gravity* by Gwyneth Lewis, published by Bloodaxe Books, 1998. Reprinted by permission of Bloodaxe Books.

Lumsden, Roddy. "Always," "An Older Woman," "Piquant," and "The Man I Could Have Been," from *The Book of Love* by Roddy Lumsden, published by Bloodaxe Books, 2000. Reprinted by permission of Bloodaxe Books.

Maxwell, Glyn. "The Poem Recalls the Poet" from *The Nerve* by Glyn Maxwell, published by Picador Press, 1992. Reprinted by permission of the author. "My Turn" and "Helene and Heloise" from *The Boys at Twilight: Poems 1990–1995* by Glyn Maxwell, published by Bloodaxe Books, UK, 2000 and Houghton Mifflin, USA, 2000. Copyright © 1990, 1992, 2000 by Glyn Maxwell. Reprinted by permission of the author and Houghton Mifflin Company. All rights reserved.

McKendrick, Jamie. "Ancient History," "Sky Nails," "Six Characters in Search of Something," and "The One-Star" from *Sky Nails: Selected Poems* by Jamie McKendrick, published by Faber & Faber Ltd., 2000. Reprinted by permission of Faber & Faber Ltd.

Motion, Andrew. "The Lines" and "The Letter" from *Dangerous Play: Poems 1974–1984* by Andrew Motion, published by Penguin Press, 1985. Reprinted by permission of Peters Fraser & Dunlop on behalf of Andrew Motion. "A Wall," "A Glass of Wine," and "Mythology" from *Public Property* by Andrew Motion, published by Faber & Faber Ltd., 2003. Reprinted by permission of Faber & Faber Ltd.

O'Brien, Sean. "Cousin Coat," "After Laforgue," and "The Amateur God" from *Cousin Coat: Selected Poems 1976–2001* by Sean O'Brien, published by Picador Press, 2002. Reprinted by permission of Macmillan, London, UK.

Oswald, Alice. "April," "Bike Ride on a Roman Road," "Sea Sonnet," "Wedding," and "Prayer" from *The Thing in the Gap-stone Stile* by Alice Oswald, published by Oxford University Press, 1996. Reprinted by permission of Peters Fraser & Dunlop on behalf of Alice Oswald.

Padel, Ruth. "On the Line" from *Summer Snow* by Ruth Padel, published by Hutchinson. Reprinted by permission of The Random House Group Ltd. "Skin" from *Fusewire* by Ruth Padel, published by Chatto & Windus, 1996. "Tinderbox" from *Rembrandt Would Have Loved You* by Ruth Padel, published by Chatto & Windus, 1998. Reprinted by permission of The Random House Group Ltd. "Angel" and "The Starling" from *Angel*, published by Bloodaxe Books, 1993. Reprinted by permission of Ruth Padel.

Paterson, Don. "The White Lie" and "St Brides: Sea-Mail" copyright 2001 by Don Paterson. Reprinted from *The White Lie* with the permission of Graywolf Press. "Imperial" from *God's Gift to Women* by Don Paterson, published by Faber & Faber Ltd. Reprinted by permission of Faber & Faber Ltd.

Reading, Peter. Excerpt from "Stet" from *Stet: Collected Poems 2* by Peter Reading, published by Bloodaxe Books, 1996. "Salopian" from *Work in Regress: Collected Poems 3: Poems 1997–2003* by Peter Reading, published by Bloodaxe Books, 2003. Reprinted by permission of Bloodaxe Books.

Reid, Christopher. "A Whole School of Bourgeois Primitives" from *Arcadia*, published by Ondt & Gracehoper, reprinted by permission of Christopher Reid. "What the Uneducated Old Woman Told Me" from *Katerina Brac* by Christopher Reid, published by Faber & Faber Ltd., 1985. "In the Echoey Tunnel" from *In the Echoey Tunnel* by Christopher Reid, published by Faber & Faber Ltd., 1991. "Mermaids Explained" and "Fetish" from *Expanded Universes* by Christopher Reid, published by Faber & Faber Ltd., 1996. Reprinted by permission of Faber & Faber Ltd.

Robertson, Robin. "Fall" and "Wedding the Locksmith's Daughter" from *Slow Air* by Robin Robertson, published by Macmillan, London, UK, 2002. "The Immoralist," "Fugue for Phantoms," and "Artichoke" from *A Painted Field* by Robin Robertson, published by Macmillan, London, UK, 1999. Reprinted by permission of Macmillan, London, UK and Harcourt Press.

Rouse, Anne. "Testament" and "The Anaesthetist" from *Timing* by Anne Rouse, published by Bloodaxe Books, 1997. "Faith Healers" and "Memo to Auden" from *Sunset Grill* by Anne Rouse, published by Bloodaxe Books, 1993. All reprinted by permission of Bloodaxe Books.

Shapcott, Jo. "Muse," "My Life Asleep," "Motherland," "The Mad Cow in Love," and "Phrase Book" from *Her Book: Poems 1988–1998* by Jo Shapcott, published by Faber & Faber Ltd., 1999. Reprinted by permission of Faber & Faber Ltd.

❦ *Contents*

Preface

Every so often one reads a piece lamenting the state of poetry today and maintaining how much better things were in the past when there were still great poets among us and masses of people who read poetry. The message of this most dubious claim is that everyone who hasn't been paying attention and reading poetry for the last few decades is to be congratulated for their foresight since there's nothing worth reading anymore. That there are lousy poems written today should come as no surprise to anyone. Most poems in any historical period range from awful to mediocre. What matters, and what continues to be true, despite such dire prognosis, is that memorable poetry continues to be written, as this anthology of *New British Poetry* clearly shows.

Until thirty years ago, one could still find ample selections of British poetry in North American schoolbooks. I recall touring high schools in Arizona, New Mexico, and Texas in 1970 on behalf of the National Endowment for the Arts and being surprised to find poems by Tennyson, Kipling, Hardy, Belloc, Sassoon, Bridges, and hardly any Americans beyond Longfellow, Poe, and Frost. Being asked to read and explain A. E. Housman to Papago High School students in the Sonora Desert struck me as an absurdity worthy of a Dadaist cabaret. One forgets how stubbornly Anglophile and oblivious to native writing teachers of English were in the past. Most American poetry, and that includes Whitman, Dickinson, Pound, Williams, and e.e. cummings, was considered ill-mannered and unsuitable for young people. When I was in college in the 1950s, Modernism was regarded with suspicion. There was a cult of Eliot and his "Waste Land," but that was as far as it went. My professors didn't approve of a revolution in taste. For them, there was nothing wrong with Victorian-sounding poems and traditional meters. What they liked about the British was their reluctance to innovate. For us, who were then beginning to write poetry, their enthusiasm made as much sense as being told to ignore the movies and jazz since they are too American.

Reacting to such views, the poets of my generation, and I imagine other readers of poetry, began to ignore what went on in Britain. Philip Larkin's magnificent poetry was not widely read; Geoffrey Hill's even less so. Then, there was Ted Hughes, better known as the husband and reputed tormentor of Sylvia Plath than as a poet in his own right. The other poets from Britain, which one occasionally encountered in magazines and anthologies, seemed tame and conventional when compared to poets from France, Germany, Spain, Eastern Europe, and South America, who were becoming widely available in translations in North America.

The rediscovery of British poetry on this continent in the last few years has a lot to do with the popularity of Irish poetry. Seamus Heaney, Paul Muldoon, John Montague, Derek Mahon, and several others had books published in this country and made themselves even more familiar to readers by giving numerous readings. If the Irish poets were so good, one thought, then what about poets in the British Isles? Like anyone who develops a sudden interest in a subject, I rushed over to my university library and borrowed books and anthologies of recent British poetry. I was embarrassed to have been unaware of such good writing.

It was contemporary North American poetry that I now found wanting. Compared to the British, a lot of what I saw in our magazines and books struck me as formulaic. The favorite kind of poem was a first-person, realistic narrative that told of some momentous or perfectly trivial experience. It was written in free verse often barely distinguished from prose. Audacious flights of the imagination and use of metaphor were rare. In the age of political correctness and the ever-growing lists of forbidden words, topics, and attitudes, irony and wit became suspect. And so did humor. The chief strategy of these poems was to conceal that they were poems by avoiding anything that seemed too imaginative or too irreverent. I'm generalizing, of course, and leaving out many North American poets who went on doing fine and inventive work, but it did appear to me that we were afflicted by a kind of smug provincialism that only a knowledge of what the poets were doing elsewhere could cure.

New British Poetry is hopefully that kind of curative book. It introduces, to North American readers, thirty-six poets from England, Scotland, and Wales. To make it as current as possible, Don Paterson and I decided to include only poets born after 1945 who have had at least two books published. Aside from that constraint, our plan was simply to read a lot of poetry and pick out the poems we like. Most of the time we were in full agreement since certain poets and poems clearly stood out and made it hard to lose sight of them. We also had occasional divergences of opinion. I'd complain that the style of some poem would be too familiar to North American readers or that its allusions would be incomprehensible to them. Inevitably, the question of what made British poetry different from North American poetry kept coming up. Is it the tone, the language, the subject matter, or the seemingly unshakable devotion to rhyme and meter? It is all of these and more. Without question, British poets are far more at home in their long poetic tradition than North American poets are and can ever be. For that very reason, their use of language is more self-conscious, more varied, and more hedonistic. The great British and Irish poets are voluptuaries of words, and North Americans rarely are.

Emerson's limitless faith in the power of the individual to make a new beginning, reinventing everything from his identity to the art of poetry, has had few takers in Britain. Consequently, their poets are less egocentric than ours, who love the first-person pronoun more than anything else in the world. American poems may probe psychological, philosophical, religious, and aesthetic issues, but they rarely show much awareness of history, economics, and politics. As a nation with a utopian bent, Americans prefer to dwell on the future rather than on the past. We are wary of traditions, closed intellectual systems, and ideas that do not come from experience. Intellectually, we tend to be autodidacts. All our great poets—and that goes for Whitman too—have been loners in search of an audience. In contrast, the poets in this anthology assume that they are part of a tradition, addressing a community that may neglect them now and then, but is there nevertheless.

Good poetry has a way of eluding even the most credible generalizations and critical labels. Despite everything I've said so far, *New British Poetry* is still a book of distinct individual voices. It displays an astonishing range of styles and an equal number of ways in which a poem can succeed. The poems in this anthology prove wrong any dogmatic aesthetic position, formalist or avant-garde, which claims to be in the possession of the ingredients and the recipe out of which superior poems are made. Most of the poets here are scavengers, free to appropriate what they need from very different kinds of poetries. The eclecticism of American poetry probably had something to do with that since living with contradictions is our national specialty. Whatever the case may be, the originality and sheer mastery to be found in this anthology is bound to restore anyone's belief in literature. If you haven't read Carol Ann Duffy, Simon Armitage, Michael Hofmann, Jo Shapcott, Alice Oswald, Christopher Reid, Gillian Allnutt, and Jamie McKendrick—to name only a few poets included here—your life, I'm tempted to say, has not been as interesting as it deserves to be. The purpose of this anthology is to remedy that without further delay.

Charles Simic

Introduction

I

British poetry is different from North American poetry. This essay is an attempt firstly to describe that difference; to give some description of the current UK scene and its schisms; to discuss the threat currently presented by the Postmoderns and their general ubiquity, and give some defence of 'Mainstream' practise; and to give a brief account of how this book was put together. All this, I should hastily add, comes from one very partisan—if not, I hope, wholly unreliable—witness. However one-sided an affair certain readers may find it, I can reassure them I have even less talent for the disinterested overview.

Some cultural commentators on the other side of the Atlantic still talk—on those rare occasions they do talk about such things—as if UK poetry were still stuck in some Georgian or Victorian timewarp. The implication is always that our poetry, somehow, either failed to keep pace with the rest of the English-speaking world in its development of the Modernist vision, or that there was something too fragile in our national temperament for the revolution it proposed; whatever Oedipal psychodrama continues to fuel this prejudice has long ceased to be interrogated.

Understandably stung by this, certain British critics have perhaps devoted too much energy to emphasising the similarities between UK and US poetries, and have gone to great pains to point out that we too have our Postmoderns, radicals, and experimentalists. It might have been less disingenuous, however, to concede that there was a grain of truth in this perception of us: the majority of the poetry actually *read* in the UK tends, quite simply, to demonstrate an allegiance to more traditional ideas of form and poetic closure than its more freewheeling, loose-lined, and open-ended North American equivalent—and perhaps also to the pure lyric, in the simplest and neutral sense of an abiding interest in the old song-forms.

The reason is fairly straightforward: Modernism fed into British poetry as a new, invigorating tributary to the river of the old tradition. In the main (that *main* we will soon have to define), it did not present itself as the revolutionary alternative it was for the US, with its concomitant assertion of cultural independence. The new formal and imaginative possibilities won by Eliot and Pound were, in the work of Auden, McNeice, and their school, already maturely assimilated by the 1930s—and Pound's more extreme call-to-arms in the later Cantos largely ignored. True, there was a black spot in the 1940s and early '50s, when the florid operatics of Dylan Thomas and a sudden and belated acquaintance with Stevens's *Harmonium* proved immediately fatal to several smaller talents (who failed to remember that the greats are great *despite* their stylistic excesses, not because of them); it also proved briefly detrimental to some very considerable ones, notably W. S. Graham and Norman McCaig. But for the most part, the new and the old came fairly quickly to a happy accommodation. As a result, there has never been the need for such brutal correctives as the 'New Formalist' movement in the UK. (Rather sweetly, the editor of a Scottish magazine with a vaguely formal bias received a letter a couple of years ago from an American poet offering his congratulations on the fact that the New Formalism had finally 'reached' Scotland.) New Formalism tends to be regarded by the majority of informed UK readers as every bit as bizarre a poetic strategy as those proposed by the Postmoderns and the L=A=N=G=U=A=G=E poets; primarily since they both appear to engage seriously with the false and very un-British paradigm of artistic progress—and even less palatably, to provide the adherents of either school a way of indicating a conservative or radical political allegiance. In contrast, then, the course of 'mainstream' poetry over the last century in the UK can be read as a relatively seamless evolution.

Mainstream: a river with tributaries. This, for better or worse, is a mainstream anthology. I'd like to see the word reclaimed from our detractors, though to do so, we should first make some attempt at a definition. In the US, one might caricature the mainstream as that broad swathe of poets who have strung their elegant steps together between the clumping clog-dance of the New Formalists from the school of Yvor Winters onwards, and the neurotic ballet of the Postmoderns, from the later Cantos and the school of Charles Olson onwards: i.e., from that pool of writers who would include Roethke, Lowell, and Bishop to Anthony Hecht, James Merrill, Adrienne Rich, Louise Glück, Gertrude Schnackenberg, C. K. Williams, Jorie Graham, Marilyn Hacker, Charles Simic, Mark Doty, and the apparently unforgivably popular Billy Collins. In the UK, the mainstream has been shaped and narrowed by the closing banks of that cheery and generally none-too-clever verse of recognition humour or undisguised moral exhortation; and by the Postmoderns on the other—and how strenuously Left—bank. However, as I hope this book will show, it has been narrowed to a fairly furious and articulate torrent.

Many of the poets in this book would, I suspect, despise the vanilla overtones of the word 'mainstream'. Worse—for those of us from poorer or working-class backgrounds, the news that you were going to dedicate your life to writing serious verse was received by the community with the same panic as might be your departure for Bader-Meinhof or a transexual circus. The idea of us being described as 'mainstream' anything still fills us with a kind of demonically unbalanced hilarity. These misgivings apart, though, it still seems the most accurate designation available.

While this book will be wrongly interpreted by some as putting itself forward as a corrective to the Postmodern revisionism of such recent anthologies as Keith Tuma's controversial *Oxford Book of British Verse*, it is, nonetheless, an alternative. However unrepresentative an account some will rightly feel *New British Poetry* to be, it can claim to be a more accurate map in at least the following way: all the poets collected here have been drawn from the set of British poets who still sell books to a general—i.e., non-practising and non-academic—readership. This is not for one moment to deny the importance of those other readerships. However, a poetry which has lost its general audience will, before long, start to smack of the thesis or the in-house memorandum; it will have suffered, whichever way you cut it, a serious cultural demotion.

For this reason, British poetry is occasionally described as 'populist'. This tends to mean no more than that it actively seeks an audience, often uses traditional forms, and considers itself primarily a kind of public art (with all the obligations to 'entertain', in the widest sense, that implies, whatever private meditations or epiphanies lie behind it). Popular, though, it isn't. By the standards of almost all other forms of literature, our sales are poor—perhaps a couple of thousand or a few hundred per book. Compared with the novel, poetry tends to enjoy very little in the way of support from publicity and marketing departments, bookstore reps, and the booksellers themselves; when these books do sell, they tend to do so largely by recommendation in the press or by word of mouth. This pays the books, I think, a considerable compliment.

This dwindling readership should not be interpreted (as has been the frequent diagnosis) as a sign that the non-metropolitans, the working classes, the ethnic minorities, or—heaven help us—'the kids' find poetry irrelevant and inaccessible. These groups are disenfranchised in many more serious ways than their mere alienation from contemporary literature, which is a only a side-symptom of a far more broad and concerted cultural indifference. As far as poetry itself is concerned, the news is far worse: it's a sign that poetry's own natural constituency has itself been alienated and lost along the way. By this I mean simply a literate and educated readership capable of responding to the demands the average contemporary poem asks of them. (Contrary to the persistent liberal dogma—'middle', in the UK, is now a class almost as frequently attained as inherited.) Lest some misread this as an argument for cultural elitism—of *course* poetry must be allowed to reach the poorer inner cities, the prisons and the factory floors; though when it does, it inevitably arrives via some patronising mediation, some strategy intended to make it 'easier': a visit from a performance poet, or a themed workshop, or a poster campaign with the dumbest, shortest poem the committee can find, set in 50-point bold; rarely anything so straightforward as restocking the school library, or handing out books to leave lying around the canteen. But to have made, in the course of our numerous awareness-raising campaigns, no direct appeal to the serious-fiction-reading, theatregoing, art-movie-viewing public—i.e., one already receptive to some level of difficulty or complexity in the art they enjoyed—was surely a grievous error.

At the other end of the scale, the potential audience for British poetry is further attenuated by the indifferent and sometimes catastrophic teaching of poetry in schools, and the consequent failure to develop a new generation of readers. Despite the fact that the poem is the only art form that you can appropriate wholesale, and then carry around in your head in its original form, the only art whose every element of composition also performs some mnemonic function—the practice of learning of poems by heart has all but disappeared; one still hears it regularly decried as if it were some kind of Victorian torment. But what greater gift could you devise for a child than a piece of high art that's literally theirs to keep forever? There are, of course, pockets of articulate resistance in the teaching profession (and a great deal of sterling educational work is done by both the British Poetry Society and Poetry Book Society); but such poetry as is taught is mostly imparted with little enthusiasm or understanding. At secondary level the discussion of poetry tends to take place only in the context of rudimentary critical analysis, with its ignorant and misplaced obsession with 'meaning'—'meaning' being something the poet has gone out of their clever way to obscure but, through some quixotic literary courtesy, left behind enough clues to allow the reader to partially decode it.

What, in the end, has been bargained away is the idea that a great poem has some intrinsic cultural value that need not be validated by any other means than its simple *reading*. Poetry is lousy decoration, a lousy way of carrying information, mostly a lousy collaborative partner, and is good for very little but itself. It should perhaps be no surprise, in our ultra-utilitarian age, that it has been among the first casualties.

What we do have in the UK, however, is a media still prepared to support the art. We may sometimes carp about the content and presentation, but this carping is a real luxury; poetry still has considerable popular exposure in the UK. We have a couple of national radio programs dedicated solely to poetry, and several arts magazine programs which feature and review it regularly; we can still rely on the majority of our books to be reviewed in the press, eventually; National Poetry Day and the various award ceremonies still generate considerable media coverage; and when Tony Harrison, or the current Poet Laureate, Andrew Motion, writes an anti-war poem condemning UK and US foreign policy, it appears the next day on the front page of one of the biggest dailies. (We must set against this the somehow terribly millennial spectacle of '100 Poets Against the War'—eventually boosted to around 1,500 Poets Against the War, which would seem to undermine the usefulness of the designation 'poet', but no matter—whose strategy, in the end, was to suggest we flood the intrays of our politicians with thousands of unread e-books. Again, reinforcing the idea that poetry itself could be of no *use*, but in sufficient bulk might be employed as a kind of electronic gunge.) There is still a powerful sense in the UK that, despite having lost much of its core readership, poetry can and should matter. Mercifully it seems that the urge to be assuaged or comforted or inspired or galvanised into action by a poem will be hardwired in the human brain for a lot longer than those few generations whose dereliction almost seems like a deliberate attempt to destroy it.

II

One flourishing group, though, would be happy to see the Mainstream disappear overnight, were it not for the fact that their treasured outsider status would then be wholly undermined. I refer, of course, to the aforementioned Postmoderns. (The North American reader is invited to think also of their own Postmoderns for the next few pages; I suspect most of what follows will apply equally well.) They are unrepresented here. While any assessment of their individual merits would have been both a more and less tolerant affair than what follows, unlike the Mainstream, they have gone to great lengths to present themselves as a distinct tribe—one unified by the usual tactics, principally the systematic denigration of those unlike themselves. It therefore seems fair to attempt some rough adumbration of their common aesthetic; more importantly, I think this will be especially useful in throwing the work and working practise of the UK Mainstream into some relief.

Amongst the UK Postmoderns are a handful of attractive voices who—had they not felt obliged to continually affect the terminal seriousness and atonality of the Po-mo School Song (as we know, even their play must be serious; *especially* their play)—would surely have flourished in the Mainstream. Mostly, though, their work is incomprehensible. One can no longer say 'incomprehensible rubbish', for incomprehension is no longer the undesirable reader-response it used to be. Incomprehension now has its aficionados, its exegetes, and its champions, who are able to detect as many shades of confusion as Buddhists do the absolute. By 'incomprehension' I don't mean a reaction to 'difficulty' or 'strangeness'; strangeness and difficulty abound in the Mainstream. I refer to that special category of difficulty *whose sensible interpretation or interpretations cannot be confirmed or validated by the text to any satisfactory degree*; and those strangenesses that cannot even be identified as such, because they have no unexceptional context. Their oft-repeated aim that the work should 'involve the reader in the production of meaning' sounds like a novel formulation; it is, of course, the identical aim of the Mainstream, who see the reader as equal collaborator in the creation of the poem. The work of the Postmoderns *delegates* the production of meaning to the reader, their poetry being largely derelict in its responsibility to aid it. The reader is alone. For those of us quickly bored by our own company, the result is work that can be objectively described as extremely boring.

The Modernists were frustrated by the limitations of poetic diction and the received forms; the epigones of the great Modernists were oppressed by metre; now the Postmodern poet finds himself bound hand and foot by finite meaning. Anything short of absolute polysemy is in danger, apparently, of limiting the interpretative possibilities of the text. (And worse—of casting the reader in a role subordinate to that of the poet. This latter point is perhaps the more crucial, since, besides the captive audience of their students, the Postmoderns only have other Postmoderns as their readers.) As a result, one halfway comprehensible line will stand out, and is often hailed as, an epiphany, a wisdom, or a great literary bravery.

It is also painfully apparent that far too few of them—on the evidence of such useful surveys as Denise Riley's "Poets on Writing"—have anything approaching what the Mainstream would recognise as a real compositional procedure, i.e., some subjective way of verifying their own line-to-line success, and hence its possible reciprocal success in the mind of the reader. No: they have systems. But if there's a common aesthetic that could be identified in *New British Poetry*, it's this: these poems, we believe, make a honest attempt to generate the literal or argumentative context by which they are to be understood. (Less an aesthetic, I'd propose, and more an act of human courtesy.) A fact too often unappreciated is that *lineation alone* indicates the presence of figure. The line's falling short of the right margin—its leaving so much white space—advertises the fact that *this is a poem*; the poem, even in the understanding of children, being a small thing that stands for a bigger thing, and possessing a deeper or broader significance than its simple prose sense might first suggest. In other words the reader, at the mere confrontation with the line, has already begun to create a fruitful difficulty for themselves, to *read in*.

The poets in *New British Poetry*, I believe, understand this relationship and calculate for it; they attempt to reward the reader for their investment. And since the poem is an act of collusion, the superimposition of a new intelligence and life-experience on the poem will result in an unique interference pattern of agreement and ambiguity for each new reader. 'Difficulty', then, is twice written into the contract—once by the reader, who is already at work unpacking the freight of the poem, whether it exists or not; and again by the poet, who is trying to shock the reader into a brief moment of wakefulness by saying something original, something they had not said before, in a way they believe no one had said before . . . how could such a statement be anything other than initially unfamiliar? Given this, the wilful addition of further confusion and disorientation seems an odd project, and an effortlessly easy one to pursue. Difficulty and figure, in the traditional lyric poem, are where the differences of interpretation will lie. These very ambiguities often grant the reader the freedom to have that part of the poem *they have grounded in finite literal sense* find some emotional resonance within their individual life-experience. 'Literal sense' playing little part in the Postmodern game, the freedoms their poets grant to the reader are almost infinite, and therefore, by any commonsense standard, worthless.

The Mainstream poets in this book are part of a long evolution, and are engaged in an open, complex and ongoing dialogue with the whole of the English lyric tradition. Despite their claims to do the same, the Postmoderns are unable to configure their relationship with this tradition, because their individual style (or, more accurately, the by-product of what they variously call 'method', 'praxis', and 'research'; though in each case it only amounts to an alternative strategy of evasion) must everywhere declare the primacy of *novelty*, since they see themselves purely in terms of a progressive vanguard—interestingly, just about the only criticism one ever hears the Postmoderns clearly articulate against the work of other Postmoderns is its failure to 'innovate'. Their plan is evolutionary succession, not cohabitation. But astonishment, in the mind of the reader, always works from the familiar to the unfamiliar, as gravity works from the ground up. There must always be a little of the quotidian to contextualise the omen, shock or surprise. The Mainstream poem attempts to hold the known and unknown in a fine internal balance; with the Postmoderns, all we get is a litany of exceptions. Not only can such a poem never surprise the reader—whatever conversations it thinks it might be engaged in, it cannot be in dialogue with *any* tradition—anything, indeed, but its own linguistic whim. The poets in this book are concerned with originality, not novelty; by which I suppose I mean, ultimately, the startling reincarnation of the old truths in the culture of the age.

In that definition of originality they find their *risk*. 'Risk' in poetry has nothing to do with the ampersand-count, or disjunctive syntax, or heaps of nonseqs, or sly allusions to Heisenberg or Heidegger, or novel systems of punctuation. Attempts at *real* originality run the risk of neither nonsense nor obscurity, but mundanity. Truly

original expression—since it must be already half-familiar to be veri-
fied as such—always runs the risk of cliché; the clear articulation
of deep emotion always runs the risk of sentimentality; and taking
the chance of being largely understood always runs the risk of being
found to be talking a pile of garbage. These are the sort of braver risks
the poets in this book run all the time, and where they occasionally
come unstuck. By contrast, the Postmoderns cannot fail in their proj-
ect; only their readers can fail them, so they need not acknowledge
anything so simple as the success-failure axis in their own practise.
Indeed such a culture could never evolve and calibrate the critical
tools necessary to measure failure in the first place: they are quick
to claim their successes and proclaim their geniuses, but (unlike
the Mainstream, who do so as a hobby) cannot point to examples of
disastrous practise within their genre, since there is little interpreted
sense to agree on that might form the basis for such a judgement.
Whereas the reader's relationship to the Mainstream poem is actually
very simple: we read; we either understand something or nothing; if
nothing, we read no further; if something, we say—*I've heard this;
this is untrue; this could've been put better;* or *this amazes, moves,
provokes, or informs me.*

The Mainstream persist with the flawed currency of sense and
idiom, knowing that this is all we have. ('Flawed' simply in the sense
of Antonio Porchia's *I know what I have given you; I do not know
what you have received.*) The Postmoderns have dispensed with the
ground of consensual meaning, and have substituted systems, pat-
terns, and the retrospective justification of the caprice for the mas-
tery of technique and form. As a result their lines are often as clean
and uncriticisable as serial composition; but their emotional palette
is so meagrely provided, it leaves them capable of nothing more than
a monotone angst, an effete and etiolated aestheticism, and a kind
of joyless wordplay that somehow passes, in their country, for wit.
Their claim to serious political engagement is wholly incompat-
ible with their clear disregard of such tediously practical matters as
exclusivity of register and reader-constituency. The Mainstream, on
the other hand, remain deeply engaged with the messy business of
communication with a real critical readership—a extremely vulner-

able situation, fraught with all manner of self-consciousness dangers: self-impersonation, second-guessing, dumbing down, sexing up, comedy, gratuitous displays of learning and allusion—in other words, the inadvertent projection and amplification of their own social neuroses, against which they must be constantly vigilant. This dialogue is open-ended; by contrast, the self-absorbed, closed-system expressionism of the Po-mos mark them out as some kind of *final* Romantic. In the end, they probably do deserve to inherit the earth, being the first literary movement to have conceived the masterstroke of eliminating the reader entirely.

At this point, I had better make it clear why I have spent such an apparently disproportionate and bad-tempered amount of time discussing this group, who, as I've said, are not even represented in this book. Like their US counterparts, the Postmoderns have now attained considerable academic influence in the UK, despite having no discernible readership beyond their own circle. In an attempt to widen that circle, they will happily omit almost every poet in this book from the surveys of the contemporary scene they present to their students; if our poets are mentioned, they tend to be dismissed on the grounds of their populism and stupidity. These must appear safe grounds: the Postmoderns sell few books to the general public, and undoubtedly think of themselves as the cleverer party. To propose—as I would for many of the writers in this book—that a 'poet' was merely a man or woman with a natural and exceptional talent for the composition of verses would have them foaming at the mouth; intelligence and systems should be enough for anyone. From which we might derive the following pretty chiasmus: the Mainstream insist on a talented minority, and a democracy of readership; the Postmoderns on an elite readership, and a democracy of talent.

If the Mainstream is to survive, it must find a way of reenlisting both the general reader *and* the Academy, whose articulate advocacy has always been its traditional means of protection when the culture and the times leave it exposed and unsupported. I hope this book offers some more evidence that the poets are still with us, waiting to be read, waiting to be reunited with that intelligent and creative reader from whom the times have conspired to divide them.

III

The criticism of anthologies generally consists, often in its entirety, of a list of unforgivable omissions; and, if the critic is feeling brave (or resigned to certain terminal enmities, or too young or old not to worry about meeting the poet in print, or very far away), the odd unforgivable inclusion. Given that, it's important, I think, to expand a little on the principles of selection Charles Simic has mention in his preface.

Firstly, despite the fact that this calls itself a British anthology, we have not included any Northern Irish poets. Despite the fact that the province remains largely under British rule, its poets—with only a few exceptions—tend to describe themselves as Irish, and not British; we felt that should be respected. The Republic has been as quick to claim them, too, and as a result they have benefited from that country's more outward-looking internationalism, and tend to enjoy a far stronger US profile than many of their counterparts on the larger island.

This book has two editors, and these are the poets we agreed on. Twelve more we disagreed on, sometimes deeply. We initially limited ourselves to twenty-five poets, found ourselves arguing for the inclusion of twenty more, and found space for eleven. We had to invoke a cut-off—otherwise this book would have been unpublishably long—and decided all poets we included had to be born after 1945, and have published at least two books by the end of 2002. Inevitably this meant some significant casualties at either end, and it might be that future editions of this book will correct this. As difficult a decision was to exclude poets who have produced their best work in either the other native tongues of these islands, or in its alternative Englishes. (One inclusion we did not agree on. I think it's good practise to exclude yourself from your own anthologies, and until now I've always followed that rule. My work is presented here against my better judgement, and at the insistence of my co-editor and my editors at Graywolf. But neither, possibly, would it have been fair to protect my own work from any criticism this introduction may invite.)

This anthology is an attempt to give some account of the work of most of the leading practitioners of the art in the UK today. It is not an attempt to represent, as other anthologies have been, the 'multiplicity of voices' to be heard in the UK. That anthology would have to be assembled by a committee, and would be the result of a duty, and not the partisan enthusiasm Charlie and I have for the subject. Besides, it has long been my own contention that 'voice'—that absurd passport we are obliged to carry through the insecurity of our age—is an extraliterary issue. The word 'voice' might usefully denote that characteristic tone whose identification can aid the reader in keeping the poems of a single poet in dialogue with one another; but more often its use is purely political. Personally, I don't believe the difference in a poet's cultural or sociosexual experience is necessarily the most significant or interesting thing about them, or even the third-most. So this is just a survey of poets; the word 'poet' being useful to the reader, ultimately, only insofar as it might identify a reliable source of good poems. Though I would hope that these days very little gets past the automatic self-scrutiny that is the most constructive product of the postfeminist and postcolonial era (though only a fool would try to negotiate their cultural blindspots—those that proceed from their being white—by *guessing* where they might lie, and then making some speculative accommodation), all an anthologist can ever do is include what they believe to be beautiful and true—or, if they can't love it, admirable in its technique and integrity of purpose.

Anyway, as you guys say, enough already. We hope this book will spawn deeper and more intimate relationships between some of these poets and you, the North American reader. We speak—don't be told otherwise—with almost exactly the same tongue, the beginning and the end of our special relationship, and where its truest commerce will take place. We offer this book in the spirit of its small and true furtherance.

Don Paterson
Kirriemuir
Scotland
July 2003

New British Poetry

∽ GILLIAN ALLNUTT

Gillian Allnutt was born in London in 1949 and lives in County Durham. Allnutt's favourite voice is in some respects quite close to that of John Burnside; like Burnside, the natural world seems to form the backdrop for many of her poems, against which Allnutt engages explicitly with social history, feminist politics, and the history of place. A poet of considerable range of tone and subject, her beautifully balanced lines—with their often strongly Anglo-Saxon diction and rhythm—deserve a wider appreciation in the UK than they have yet achieved. Though she can work within the framework of ambitious narrative sequences, hers is often a poetry of small and delightfully calculated surprises, surreal excursions, and an often highly arresting imagistic clarity.

FURTHER READING:
Lintel (Bloodaxe, 2001), *Nantucket and the Angel* (Bloodaxe, 1997)

Scheherazade

He is languid as a fed lion.
She in her salt and sackcloth gown is gone
into a wilderness of wind at noon

where the wonderful covered well of tales
is a dry waterhole
or a bell

abandoned. What is the sound at noon
of silence in a grain
of sand? It may be what is borne

by her beyond the hollowed bone of thought,
the loud elaborated heart,
the salt

and sack-
cloth shadow begging briefly at her back,
her Bedouin back.

The Silk Light of Advent

Mara sighs over the silks laid out on the rosewood windowsill.
She would rather look into the fire.
It is terribly hard to decide when the garden is dead.
In December the lake is dumb.
There are no leaves left and no wind left to stir them.
Later in life she will say that the light on the Somme was like
    that then.
Mara sighs over the skeins.
She is neither girl nor woman.
Her brother is in uniform.
There is no one left to walk with in the morning.
Her mother has always left her alone.
The newspaper's forbidden.
The angel will be embroidered, soon, by evensong.
After that there'll be no more sewing.
In the beginning needles were made of bone.
The angel will come in the afternoon.
Later in life she will know the value of precision.
At two o'clock in the afternoon she will say again and again.
Her brother will not be missing then.
He writes he is learning to smoke and polish buttons.
She will get up from the fire.
She'll walk slowly back to the windowsill.
She'll know then that the angel's hands are dumb.
The eyes are gone.
There are sockets of silk she will never embroider for him.
The lake is dry, like bone.
The angel is terribly beautiful.
She won't be able to cry.

Held To

And now a little wind but little wind and stone and green—
grave-green

the pod of flowered-
already reed

or sedge—
and now, at water's edge,

a leap and tipple—toad, alone, moves
now, reminds me of

the little tinie page,
the page

in *Matty Groves*, who ran to give the game away
on New Year's Day

and now, but for the barest grace of balladry, go I
too hurriedly

beyond
this borderland,

this little hoard of stone, pod, wind
in the hand

that would hold tipple-
still

to

Notes on living inside the lightbulb

One hundred watts blinded me.
I nestled near the warm white shell.
Furthest from the filament was not too hot.
After it blew I began to be able.
I saw the old world's end.
It was cold as I crept around.
I covered miles within the curvature of bone.
I inspected its now off-white.
I noticed the soft brown singe came off on my feet.
I left footprints on the off-white.
I was interested in my footprints.
Long I steered clear of the broken filament.
Later I saw what it was, cross-eyed, a swastika.

The Road Home

It is the road to God
that matters now, the ragged road, the wood.

And if you will, drop pebbles here and there
like Hansel, Gretel, right where

they'll shine
in the wilful light of the moon.

You won't be going back to the hut
where father, mother plot

the *cul de sac* of the world
in a field

that's permanently full
of people

looking for a festival
of literature, a fairy tale,

a feathered
nest of brothers, sisters. Would

that first world, bared now to the word
God, wade

with you, through wood, into the weald and weather
of the stars?

Simon Armitage was born in Huddersfield in 1963. He works as a writer, broadcaster, and playwright, and lectures in creative writing at Manchester Metropolitan University and the University of Iowa. Armitage, along with Carol Ann Duffy, is one of the UK's most popular poets. While this has allowed him to become a highly influential advocate for the art, it has also won him an audience sometimes less able to read his considerable sophistications. He has written some unsettlingly unsentimental poems which address the working-class experience, and through these he seems to have inherited the older Tony Harrison's mantle as unofficial laureate of the North; however they form only a very small part of Armitage's prolific and highly varied output. Armitage is a poet of terrific rhetorical power and control, and his range extends from the most delicate lyric to scorching, breakneck litanies, from concrete poems to popular song.

FURTHER READING:
Selected Poems (Faber & Faber, 2001)

Very Simply Topping Up the Brake Fluid

Yes, love, that's why the warning light comes on. Don't
panic. Fetch some universal brake fluid
and a five-eighths screwdriver from your toolkit
then prop the bonnet open. Go on, it won't

eat you. Now, without slicing through the fan-belt
try and slide the sharp end of the screwdriver
under the lid and push the spade connector
through its bed, go on, that's it. Now you're all right

to unscrew, no, clockwise, you see it's Russian
love, back to front, that's it. You see, it's empty.
Now, gently with your hand and I mean gently,
try and create a bit of space by pushing

the float-chamber sideways so there's room to pour,
gently does it, that's it. Try not to spill it, it's

corrosive: rusts, you know, and fill it till it's
level with the notch on the clutch reservoir.

Lovely. There's some Swarfega in the office
if you want a wash and some soft roll above
the cistern for, you know. Oh don't mind him, love,
he doesn't bite. Come here and sit down Prince. Prince!

Now, where's that bloody alternator? Managed?
Oh any time, love. I'll not charge you for that
because it's nothing of a job. If you want
us again we're in the book. Tell your husband.

Poem

And if it snowed and snow covered the drive
he took a spade and tossed it to one side.
And always tucked his daughter up at night.
And slippered her the one time that she lied.

And every week he tipped up half his wage.
And what he didn't spend each week he saved.
And praised his wife for every meal she made.
And once, for laughing, punched her in the face.

And for his mum he hired a private nurse.
And every Sunday taxied her to church.
And he blubbed when she went from bad to worse.
And twice he lifted ten quid from her purse.

Here's how they rated him when they looked back:
sometimes he did this, sometimes he did that.

The Tyre

Just how it came to rest where it rested,
miles out, miles from the last farmhouse even,
was a fair question. Dropped by hurricane
or aeroplane perhaps for some reason,
put down as a cairn or marker, then lost.
Tractor-size, six or seven feet across,
it was sloughed, unconscious, warm to the touch,
its gashed, rhinoceros, sea-lion skin
nursing a gallon of rain in its gut.
Lashed to the planet with grasses and roots,
it had to be cut. Stood up it was drunk
or slugged, wanted nothing more than to slump,
to spiral back to its circle of sleep,
dream another year in its nest of peat.
We bullied it over the moor, drove it,
pushed from the back or turned it from the side,
unspooling a thread in the shape and form
of its tread, in its length and in its line,
rolled its weight through broken walls, felt the shock
when it met with stones, guided its sleepwalk
down to meadows, fields, onto level ground.
There and then we were one connected thing,
five of us, all hands steering a tall ship
or one hand fingering a coin or ring.

Once on the road it picked up pace, free-wheeled,
then moved up through the gears, and wouldn't give
to shoulder-charges, kicks; resisted force
until to tangle with it would have been
to test bone against engine or machine,
to be dragged in, broken, thrown out again
minus a limb. So we let the thing go,
leaning into the bends and corners,

balanced and centred, riding the camber,
carried away with its own momentum.
We pictured an incident up ahead:
life carved open, gardens in half, parted,
a man on a motorbike taken down,
a phone-box upended, children erased,
police and an ambulance in attendance,
scuff-marks and the smell of burning rubber,
the tyre itself embedded in a house
or lying in the gutter, playing dead.
But down in the village the tyre was gone,
and not just gone but unseen and unheard of,
not curled like a cat in the graveyard, not
cornered in the playground like a reptile,
or found and kept like a giant fossil.
Not there or anywhere. No trace. Thin air.

Being more in tune with the feel of things
than science and facts, we knew that the tyre
had travelled too fast for its size and mass,
and broken through some barrier of speed,
outrun the act of being driven, steered,
and at that moment gone beyond itself
towards some other sphere, and disappeared.

The Dead Sea Poems

And I was travelling lightly, barefoot
over bedrock, then through lands that were stitched
with breadplant and camomile. Or was it

burdock. For a living I was driving
a river of goats towards clean water,
when one of the herd cut loose to a cave

on the skyline. To flush it out, I shaped
a sling from a length of cotton bandage,
or was it a blanket, then launched a rock

at the target, which let out a racket—
the tell-tale sound of man-made objects.
Inside the cave like a set of skittles

stood a dozen caskets, and each one gasped—
a little theatrically perhaps—
when opened, then gave out a breath of musk

and pollen, and reaching down through cool sand
I found poems written in my own hand.
Being greatly in need of food and clothing,

and out of pocket, I let the lot go
for twelve times nothing, but saw them again
this spring, on public display, out of reach

under infra-red and ultra-sonic,
apparently worth an absolute packet.
Knowing now the price of my early art

I have gone some way towards taking it all
to heart, by bearing it all in mind, like
praying, saying it over and over

at night, by singing the whole of the work
to myself, every page of that innocent,
everyday, effortless verse, of which this

is the first.

JOHN ASH

John Ash was born in Manchester in 1948 and has lived in New York since 1985. A poet of great imaginative range and beautifully relaxed delivery, Ash often favours the pose of postmodern flaneur. Although Ash's greater debt is perhaps to French poetry, his jazzy urbanities and dazzling intellectual sheen can't help but put one in mind of Frank O'Hara, his manic cinematography of Ashbery; in the end, though, Ash is one of the very few poets to have forged a genuinely transatlantic voice—perhaps proving that actually living on both sides of the pond is the only way to acquire one.

FURTHER READING:
Selected Poems (Carcanet, 1996)

The Ungrateful Citizens

It occurs to me that I would like to write a poem about Naples.
Perhaps I have always wanted to do this, and only realized it just a
    moment ago,
but, alas, I have never been to Naples, and yet my desire to write
    about the place
becomes more insuperable by the second. I become convinced that
    my writing desk
is on the same latitude as Naples: I have only to lean back in
    my chair,
and I incline toward the city of my dreams, and in my dreams
    my feet
rest in Manhattan while my hair rustles against the wharves
    of Naples,
and the wharves are bristling with galleons, feluccas, sloops, and
    schooners,
and how blue the sea on which they sway and jostle, how blue
    the sky
above them, except for some small clumps of cloud so white they
    are like
roses that have seen ghosts! And one could wander forever in
    the streets

that are as narrow and crooked as the wrinkles on the face of a wise
    and beautiful old woman.
Here all the shop signs are like the titles of arias by Alessandro
    Scarlatti.
The streets and squares are always busy, yet no one is ever too
    hurried:
at the slightest opportunity a man or woman of Naples will sit
    down with you
on some weathered marble doorstep and engage you in the most
    animated conversation
concerning art or politics, your origins, their mother, the latest
    songs or scandals.
A citizen of Naples will say: 'Oh, you are from Brooklyn? I have a
    cousin there.
He tells me it is a very beautiful place.' He will say this out of
    pure courtesy.
In no other city have I seen so many fragrant pots of flowering
    bergamot,
or such luscious leaves of basil, or so many balconies overhung by
    noble bosoms.
In the late afternoon it is customary for singers to leave the
    opera house,
and go about their business in full costume: here is the Orfeo of
    Monteverdi
haggling over the price of some pomegranates, and over there
    Dona Elvira
is sipping an espresso in a café while sharing a secret with a
    dishevelled Desdemona;
Don Carlos leaves a haberdashers in a fury, while Pinkerton enters
    a tobacconist's,
and Melisande (still in character) weeps beside a baroque public
    fountain
and here is Poppaea, and Dido, and Ariadne, and Judith, and Violetta
and there goes Madame Butterfly's child eating a fruit like a
    setting sun

as he saunters down toward the waterfront. There, on the broad
    esplanade,
with its prodigious statuary, many restaurants are to be found,
and they are at once elegant and welcoming. During the heat of
    the day
their cool marble floors and gently rotating fans are a delight,
and in the evenings entire families go out to dine dressed in the
    finest clothes,
and how charming are the pink and white dresses of the young girls,
who resemble gardenias or oleander flowers as they settle lightly
    into their seats.
The families are very large, which is why the restaurants are
    so spacious—
stretching away into shimmering distances in which the fans stir
    the torpid fronds of palms—
and why the menus are so long and as varied as the colours
    of autumn.
Here the generations are nightly conjoined in perfect amity,
and even shy lovers may find corners in which to commune
    unnoticed
except by some musician, who wishes only to urge their love
    forward
from a tactful distance. The food, it goes without saying, is
    delicious.
In Naples the taxi drivers have, of necessity, become expert in
    the negotiation
of long flights of stairs resembling formalised cascades,
and the buses constantly circling monuments to heroes of the
    Risorgimento
seem to be dancing a siciliano as the sunlight rebounds from their
    windows
and shatters against the high walls of tenements. Beyond those
    walls, however,
in some lightless courtyard a skinny child is crying under lines
    of washing

that repeat, day after day, the same doleful sentence, and I am
    reminded
that this is the city in which songbirds were once blinded so they
    would sing
more poignantly in churches on saints' days, beating against the
    domes and the vaults . . .
and it seems that despite the cheerful beggarwomen and roguish
    merchants
bowed down by enormous, tufted turbans, despite the bravado
of virile gentlemen dressed like eighteenth-century courtesans that
    I had imagined for my Naples,
despite the numberless palaces and paintings, the extravagant
    churches, theatres,
and festivals, and the flowers that perfume even the poorest
    quarters,
it seems that all but the richest and most conservative of citizens
    cannot wait to leave my Naples.
They wish to go to the north or far to the west. They crowd the
    quays and the airport lounges,
and exhibit the horrible condition of their skin, the rags they are
    forced to wear,
the few possessions they drag behind them like so many coffins
    filled with stones.
They glare at me and say: 'This is not Naples. This is a place on
    which the world has turned its back.
A cloud of lies covers it. The mansions that you saw are hovels, the
    churches tin shacks,
the parks and gardens vegetable plots and stony fields in which we
    scratch for a living.
And this is not even the site of wars and massacres, only a place of
    ordinary wretchedness.
No, we cannot be the amorous ballet the tourist requires for
    a backdrop—
O take us away, perhaps to the *island of fragrant grasses* mentioned
    in a fragment of Petronius.'

The Sky My Husband

The sky my husband
The sky my wife
The sky my country and my grief
The sky my courtyard and my fountain
The sky my hyacinth
The sky my flock of birds and my guitar
The sky my kitchen and my knives
The sky my winter coat my summer shirt
The sky my balloon my acrobat
The sky my dancing-floor
The sky my café and my cinema
The sky my park and my path between the statues
The sky my garden of white trees
The sky my carousel
The sky my opera and my madrigal
The sky my actors and my theatre
The sky my wind-mill
The sky my evenings and my books
The sky my taxi my *tabac*
The sky my attic my hotel
The sky my railways and my stations
The sky my cities and my stones
The sky my head my hair my limbs
The sky my eyes my spectacles
The sky my nights my neon
The sky my balcony my garland and my mask
The sky my terrace and my tables
The sky my avenues and bridges
The sky my chandelier my Chinese lantern
The sky my roots and branches
The sky my awnings and my hope
The sky my gulfs my lakes my canyons
The sky my arches and my aqueducts in ruins

The sky my waning moon my child
The sky my rivers and cascades
The sky my forests and my solitude
The sky my castle and my flight of stairs
The sky my windows and my roofs
The sky my aerials and factory chimneys
The sky my pavilion and my tomb
The sky my incense and my hymn
The sky my journals and my magazines
The sky my violin my piano
The sky my medals and my coins
The sky my puddles and my dust
Le ciel mes feux d'artifice
The sky my scarves my hats my gloves
The sky my showers my snow my salt my sleet
The sky my mansions and my mother
The sky my diary and my photographs
The sky my cedars and my roses
The sky my face my cake of soap
The sky my memory my mountains
The sky my paper boat my autumns and my loss
The sky my palms and my Sahara
The sky my porches and my atriums
The sky my galleries my icons
The sky my radio my satellite my video
The sky my drought my famine
The sky my street-lamps my alleys and my crowds
The sky my armies and my guns my death
The sky my exile and my winters
The sky my victories and massacres
The sky my ministries my lies my parliament my eloquence
The sky my labyrinth my irony
The sky my carnation my buttonhole my bed
The sky my rondos and my boredom
The sky my flotillas and my rafts of flowers
The sky my love-affairs my comedies

The sky my theories and forgetfulness
The sky my Paris my New York my Rome
The sky great wheel of lights and colours
The sky my Venice my Vienna and my Petersburg
The sky my Alexandria
The sky my empire my provinces my people
The sky my islands and my harbours
The sky my lullaby
The sky my blood my breath my home
The sky my end

Memories of Italy

I loved the light of course
and the way the young men
flirted with each other.
I loved the light,—

the way it fell out of a sky like a painting,
or perhaps like the ground (if this
is not too paradoxical a way of
putting it) for a painting,

and the way the young men stood in the station
wearing jeans that were the colour of the sky
or the sea in a painting, jeans that revealed
the shapes of their legs which reminded me

of the statues in the square outside the station
where the light fell with such violence
their shadows were blacker than the despair of the painter
who cannot proceed with the painting: the canvas
is before him, its ground blue and blank as the sky above the station

where the young men loiter like the heroes in one of the lulls of the
    Trojan War
when lazy picnics were possible beside the calm sea, under the
    smiling sky,
and it half seems that the war will end forever, for surely they must
    all soon fall in love with each other . . .
And the painter knows his painting must be heroic, that the blue is
    not the sky
but a terrible sea a God has raised to drown the beauty of the young
    men in the marble battlefield of the station,

and he knows the painting is finished,
that it represents the envy the divine must feel
towards the human as marble must envy the sea,

and the painting is hung in the concourse of the station
and the young men drift indifferently to and fro before it:
their feet hardly seem to touch the blue marble ground.

ᘛ SUJATA BHATT

Sujata Bhatt was born in Ahmedabad in 1956, has worked in the US and Canada, and now lives in Germany. Bhatt's poetry everywhere reveals a deep engagement with the other arts. Her pose is that of the world-citizen—one she is eminently qualified to strike: her configuration of her multiple influences makes for fascinating reading, and she finds resonances and correspondences across cultures and disciplines a more circumscribed experience and vision could not. This makes her insight all the rarer and more valuable, and her translucent, weightless line cleverly disguises a rigorous technique.

FURTHER READING:
Brunizem (Carcanet, 1988), *A Colour for Solitude* (Carcanet, 2002)

શેરડી *(Shérdi)*

The way I learned
to eat sugar cane in Sanosra:
I use my teeth
to tear the outer hard *chaal*
then, bite off strips
of the white fibrous heart—
suck hard with my teeth, press down
and the juice spills out.

January mornings
the farmer cuts tender green sugar cane
and brings it to our door.
Afternoons, when the elders are asleep
we sneak outside carrying the long smooth stalks.
The sun warms us, the dogs yawn,
our teeth grow strong
our jaws are numb;
for hours we suck out the *russ*, the juice
        sticky all over our hands.

So tonight
when you tell me to use my teeth,
to suck hard, harder,
then, I smell sugar cane grass,
                    in your hair
and imagine you'd like to be
shérdi   shérdi   out in the fields
            the stalks sway
                    opening a path before us

શેરડી (Shérdi): sugar cane

Muliebrity

I have thought so much about the girl
who gathered cow-dung in a wide, round basket
along the main road passing by our house
and the Radhavallabh temple in Maninagar.
I have thought so much about the way she
moved her hands and her waist
and the smell of cow-dung and road-dust and wet canna lilies,
the smell of monkey breath and freshly washed clothes
and the dust from crows' wings which smells different—
and again the smell of cow-dung as the girl scoops
it up, all these smells surrounding me separately
and simultaneously—I have thought so much
but have been unwilling to use her for a metaphor,
for a nice image—but most of all unwilling
to forget her or to explain to anyone the greatness
and the power glistening through her cheekbones
each time she found a particularly promising
mound of dung—

What Is Worth Knowing?

That Van Gogh's ear, set free
wanted to meet the powerful nose
of Nevsky Avenue.
That Spain has decided to help
NATO. That Spring is supposed to begin
on the 21st of March.
That if you put too much salt in the *keema*
just add a few bananas.
That although the Dutch were the first
to help the people of Nicaragua they don't say much
about their history with Indonesia.
That Van Gogh collected Japanese prints.
That the Japanese considered
the Dutch to be red-haired barbarians.
That Van Gogh's ear remains full of questions
it wants to ask the nose of Nevsky Avenue.
That the vaccinations for cholera, typhoid and yellow fever
are no good—they must be improved.
That red, green and yellow are the most
auspicious colours.
That turmeric and chilli powder are good
disinfectants. Yellow and red.
That often Spring doesn't come
until May. But in some places
it's there in January.
That Van Gogh's ear left him because
it wanted to become a snail.
That east and west
meet only in the north and south—but never
in the east or west.
That in March 1986 Darwinism is being
reintroduced in American schools.

That there's a difference
between pigeons and doves, although
a ring-dove is a wood-pigeon.
That the most pleasant thing is to have a fever
of at least 101—because then the dreams aren't
merely dreams but facts.
That during a fever the soul comes out
for fresh air, that during a fever the soul bothers to
speak to you.
That tigers are courageous and generous-hearted
and never attack unless provoked—
but leopards,
leopards are malicious and bad-tempered.
That buffaloes too,
water-buffaloes that is, have a short temper.
That a red sky at night is a good sign for sailors,
for sailors . . . what is worth knowing?
What is worth knowing?

Fischerhude, 2001

Café im Rilke-Haus

Clara, your house
            is a café now—
Restored, preserved—
and named for one
            who never entered it—

Thick green, the grass in September—

Horses step out of the fog—

A stream from the Wümme
       still flows by your garden—

I drink tea and stare
       out the window—

And I have a stone in my pocket—
       a stone and an acorn—

∽ JOHN BURNSIDE

John Burnside was born in Dunfermline, Scotland, in 1955; was brought up in Corby, England; and now lives in Fife. He has a natural improvisatory fluency perhaps only shared by John Ash, Sean O'Brien, and W. N. Herbert. Burnside is resolutely a poet of the light; his radiant meditations have been perhaps the most quietly and pervasively influential voice to have emerged in British poetry in the last twenty years, and many poets have been touched by 'that Burnside thing', a kind of transparent natural-world numen; he has almost added a new colour to the palette. Burnside is also a novelist; his novels are as dark and brooding as his poems are sunlit, and clearly something in his psyche is held in balance by the two disciplines.

FURTHER READING:
The Myth of the Twin (Jonathan Cape, 1994), *The Asylum Dance* (Jonathan Cape, 2000)

Parousia

I

I could imagine a biblical presence:
a darkening of matter like this charged
sky, before the coming of the storm,
the lime trees around the station
streaming with rain,
a stiffening, a scab of pus and blood,
a wound on the air, a voice above the rooves,

—but I think, if it came, there would be
something more subtle:
a blur at the corner of vision, a trick of the light,
or the notion that things have shifted

closer: streetlamps and walls,
privet hedges, trees, the neighbour's door,
intimate, all of a sudden, and out in the dark

the animals defined and understood
—vixen and weasel, barn owl and pipistrelle—
granted their privileged moments to sleep and kill.

II

Companion self: not me, but echoes
breeding on the skin;
a half-life of touches and blows, the sub-microscopic
pattern of resurrection.
                              I knew I could squat
in the fen-smell under the hedge
or walk away through fields and timber yards
to moorhens' nests and oildrums full of rain,

but somewhere along the way
I would meet the Christ:
a tripwire; a mat of hair; an open wound;
the silver of fish blood and bone
in the whites of his eyes.

III

There were borders I never crossed:
pools of goldenrod behind the barn,
harrows and tangles of wire
immersed in weed,

the meadow beyond our road, the purple woods,
the watergall, the sub-infinity
of oatfields at dawn

—but I knew he was always present, walking away
in the warmth of the ripening grain,
dangerous, graceful, bright as a circus cat,
or the man from the high wire, come down to touch the earth,

tasting the air, how it sweetens and turns to blood
in the throat, in the new-won flesh, in the sudden body.

IV

It was less of a stream than a border:
a rill over wheat-coloured stones, then a sudden
dimming.
               And that was the place to cross,
treading the cold, my bare feet snagging a depth
of fish-skin and weed,
that was the kingdom of pike, where the body was laid
a finger's depth under the sand.

The far side was stranger's country, a half-mile away:
a back road far in the heat, a gust of wind,
cow parsley, mare's tails, a glimmer of slate in the distance,
and out in the open field, a dog-fox
pausing in its stride, to scent the air,
the only spirit I could understand
the black awareness rooted in its eyes.

A heresy, but soul becomes
conceivable, immersed in viscera,
and mind endures, in wisps of meat and bone;
at twilight, crossing the river, I always knew
something was close, but all I ever saw
was blood-warm, vivid, wholly physical:
the sparrow-hawk sweeping the air, the questing owl,
the stoat in the wall, that knows where its hunger is going.

V

All resurrections are local:
footprints bleeding away
through marsh-grass and water,

a sound you can almost hear
of the flesh renewed
in the plashing of rain
or a quick trout
breaking the stream.

For the sign I have waited to see
is happening now
and always, in this white continuum
of frost and spawn:
the blood in a tangle of thorns
where it stiffens and pales,
the hard bud splitting through ice
and the nailed palm healing.

The Old Gods

Now they are condemned
to live in cracks,
in bubbles of plaster and rust,
and spiders' webs
behind the furniture:

speaking a derelict language
to empty space,
sealed with the vapour
in bottles, closed in the blown
robins' eggs
in some abandoned loft.

Each has its given power.
Each has its hearth, its secret,
its local name,
and each has its way of learning

the skill of return,
the science of bleeding through, when anger or fear
is fuzzing the surface,
making us dizzy and whole.

ᴄ⸝ ROBERT CRAWFORD

Robert Crawford was born in Bellshill, Scotland, in 1959 and teaches at the University of St Andrews. Crawford's quick and often dandyish verse displays his love of cornucopias, collisions of register and vocabulary. He is also an academic critical powerhouse, and one of our most energetic advocates of an independent Scottish republic. His poetry is essentially celebratory and exudes an apparently boundless enthusiasm for his subjects—Scotland, family, religious faith, science—and shows a magpie instinct for the striking phrase, in whatever jargon or discipline he happens to find it. He has also written some fine poems in Scots.

FURTHER READING:
A Scottish Assembly (Chatto & Windus, 1990), *Spirit Machines* (Jonathan Cape, 1999)

The Saltcoats Structuralists

(for Douglas Cairns)

They found the world's new structure was a binary
Gleaming opposition of two rails

That never crossed but ran on parallel
Straight out of Cairo. From small boys

On Platform One who listened to the great
Schola cantorum of connecting rods

Dreamed-up by Scots-tongued engineers, they went on
To tame the desert, importing locomotives

From a distant Firth. New wives came out, and one,
Shipwrecked off Ailsa Craig, returned to Glasgow,

Caught the next boat; her servants had her wardrobe
Replaced in just four hours from the city shops.

Scotsmen among colonial expats
They learned RP, embarrassing their families

In Ayrshire villages where they talked non-stop
About biggah boilahs, crankshawfts. Nicknamed 'The Pharaohs',

They never understood the deconstruction
Visited on Empire when their reign in Egypt

Ran out of steam. They first-classed back to Saltcoats,
Post-Nasser; on slow commuter diesels

They passed the bare brick shells of loco-sheds
Like great robbed tombs. They eyed the proud slave faces

Of laid-off engineering workers, lost
In the electronics revolution. Along the prom

They'd holidayed on in childhood, with exotic walking sticks,
History in Residence, they moved

In Sophoclean raincoats. People laughed
At a world still made from girders, an Iron Age

Of Queen Elizabeths, pea-soupers, footplates,
And huge black toilet cisterns named 'St Mungo'.

Kids zapped the videogames in big arcades
Opposite Arran. Local people found

New energy sources, poems didn't rhyme.
The Pharaohs' grandchildren's accents sounded to them

Wee hell-taught ploughmen's. In slow seafront caffs
They felt poststructuralism, tanged with salt.

The Handshakes

I flinched at the handshake of a woman in labour
Through mid-contraction when you pushed our son

Down towards the forceps.
Soon his fingers curled

Possessively around my index finger
And then round yours,

Welcoming us with a reflex action
To take your hand beyond yon Labour Suite
Where you clutched me as you breathed the Entonox
And called for your own mother, who is dead.

The Result

1707–1997; for Alice

Moments after death, I found my voice
Surprising, hearing my own

Ansafone saying, 'I'm not here just now,
Please speak after the tone.'

You saw it in my eyes—release
Back to the world. More, more

You, Scotland, sea, each lost and re-elected.
I toast debatable lands, the come-go shore

Of living here. 'Thanks!' My full, bannock-smeared glass
Rises to you, our son, and our new, blonde

Daughter. We dance, in grey St Michael slippers,
Cancerless, broken out, and passed beyond.

Fiat Lux

Let there be braziers, holophotal lenses,
Polished golden flags, champagne and candles,

Let rays shine through the rose window of Chartres,
Let there be cowslips, myriad splats of rain,
Trilobites, new parliaments, red neon,
Let there be twin-stone rings and mirrorglass

Skyscrapers, glinting jumbos, Rannoch lochans
In which huge skies can touch down in the sun.

Let there be Muckle Flugga's phallic pharos,
Bug-eyed, winking tree-frogs; let there be

Grand Canyons, fireflies, tapers, tapirs, matches
Good and bad, simply to fan the flames.

Let there be lasers, Fabergé crystal eggs,
Hens' squelchy yokes, birch-bark's thin,

Diaphanous scratchiness, let there be you,
Me, son and daughter, let the Rhine

Flow through Cologne and Basle, let there be
Victoria Falls, Great Zimbabwe, hornet's wings,

Angels, cardboard, zinc, the electric brae.
Let there be both stromatolites and cows,

Llamas and zebras, dromedaries, cats,
Bens, buns and banns, let there be all,

End all, every generation, so the whole
Unknown universe be recreated

Through retinal cone and iris and religion.
As has been said before, let there be light.

Alba Einstein

When proof of Einsten's Glaswegian birth
First hit the media everything else was dropped:
Logie Baird, Dundee painters, David Hume—all
Got the big E. Physics documentaries
Became peak-viewing; Scots publishers hurled awa
MacDiarmid like an overbaked potato, and swooped
On the memorabilia: *Einstein Used My Fruitshop,*
Einstein in Old Postcards, Einstein's Bearsden Relatives.
Hot on their heels came the A. E. Fun Park,
Quantum Court, Glen Einstein Highland Malt.
Glasgow was booming. Scotland rose to its feet
At Albert Suppers where The Toast to the General Theory
Was given by footballers, panto-dames, or restaurateurs.
In the US an ageing lab-technician recorded
How the Great Man when excited showed a telltale glottal stop.
He'd loved fiddlers' rallies. His favourite sport was curling.
Thanks to this, Scottish business expanded
Endlessly. His head grew toby-jug-shaped,
Ideal for keyrings. He'd always worn brogues.
Ate bannocks in exile. As a wee boy he'd read *The Beano.*
His name brought new energy: our culture was solidly based
On pride in our hero, The Universal Scot.

↪ FRED D'AGUIAR

Fred D'Aguiar was born in London in 1960 and spent much of his childhood in Guyana; he now teaches at the University of Miami. His sharp-witted and knowing verse has often circled round questions of culture and identity. Though he has written vividly of his Guyanese roots—sometimes in a nervy and vivid patois—D'Aguiar's mature style probably owes as much to the influence of Tony Harrison and Seamus Heaney as to other Caribbean writers. Recent work has seen him tackle ambitious narrative themes and engage with more openly political subject matter; he has done this with a characteristically deft touch and sharp humour than lessens none of its impact. D'Aguiar is also a successful novelist and playwright.

FURTHER READING:
Airy Hall (Chatto & Windus, 1989), *British Subjects* (Bloodaxe, 1993)

Airy Hall Nightmare

You sleep little and light
In a bed made for two big people.
Now the springs are brands;
Now electric rings;
Now nails stacked close as bristles.

You are in this bed on the open sea
Strapped under bedding tucked in tight,
Without the strength to lift your arm,
The one with a thousand needles
Or stripped of all nerves, it's not yours.

Nose down in a pillow,
How can you shift the boulder
That is your likeness,
Greying by the second?
With sheer will? How indeed.

The Cow Perseverance

I

Here I am writing you on old newspaper against a tide of print,
In the regular spaces between lines (there are no more trees).
I've turned it upside-down to widen the gap bordering sense and
    nonsense,
For what I must say might very well sound as if it were topsy-turvy.
I put myself in your shoes (unable to recall when I last set eyes on
    a pair).
You read everything twice, then to be doubly sure, aloud,
Testing their soundness: *we wash cow's dung for its grain,*
And I feel your stomach turn; it's not much unlike collecting it
    for fuel,
Or mixed with clay to daub cracks in our shelters and renew
    door-mounds
That free us of rain, insects and spirits. They no longer drop
    the milk
We let them live for; their nights spent indoors for safe keep,
Their days tethered to a nearby post. People eye them so, they
    are fast
Becoming our cross; you'd think they'd fallen out of the sky.

II

Hunger has filled them with what I can only call compassion.
Such bulbous, watery eyes blame us for the lack of grass and worse,
Expect us to do something; tails that held the edge of windscreen
    wipers
In better days, swishing the merest irritant, a feather's even,
Let flies congregate until the stretched, pockmarked hide is them.
That's why, when you asked how things were, I didn't have to
    look far,
I thought, *Let the cow explain, its leathery tongue has run this
    geography*

Many times over; how milk turns, unseen, all at once, so lush
   pastures
Threw up savannahs. The storms are pure dust or deep inside the
   rowdiest
Among us, virtually dead and rowdy because they know it, they're
   not sure
What else to do. You fathom why, when a cow croons, we offer it
What we can't as a bribe for it to stop: *silence is perseverance.*

III

We watch its wait on meagre haunches, ruminating on what must be
Imperishable leather, some secret mantra, our dear buddha, for the
   miracle
We need; and us, with nowhere to turn, find we believe. God knows
It's a case of choosing which pot-hole in the road to ride; knowing
We export the asphalt that could fill them; knowing too the one
   thing
We make these days that is expressly ours is whipped in malarial
   water
And forced down our throats for daring to open our mouths.
Give us the cow's complicity anyday: its perfect art of being left
In peace; its till-now effortless conversion of chewy grass to milk
And its daft hoof-print, ignored for so long though clearly
   trespassing.
Then and then alone, we too can jump over the moon, without
   bloodshed.
Its raised-head and craned-neck attempt to furnish an exact account
Is a tale you and I are bound to finish, in flesh or spirit.

Sound Bite

The marines look vernal
in the studio lights,

caught in their nocturnal
amphibious landings.

They patrol Somalia
in monsoon rains and sun,
far from the familiar
snowstorm-flashflood-season.

They shake the bony stems
of withered hands which children,
women and shadowy men
offer saviours not friends.

The local militia
in customised armoury
dash for the interior
firing at anybody.

Laden relief convoys
will reach bandit terrain
where the too-long starved die
anyway watching grain;

the last of the children
grown accustomed to eating
the bark off sparse trees, then
absolutely nothing,

can't swallow. They perish.
Here even shallow graves
defeat the healthiest.
All the words for food have

become the stuff legends
spring from, or plain foreign,

as these helmeted men,
fresh-faced in fatigues,

tarpaulin topped trucks drop;
who hop and skip from jeeps,
fit and fat and so proud,
to feast our eyes is sweet.

Home

These days whenever I stay away too long,
anything I happen to clap eyes on,
(that red telephone box) somehow makes me
miss here more than anything I can name.

My heart performs a jazzy drum solo
when the crow's feet on the 747
scrape down at Heathrow. H.M. Customs . . .
I resign to the usual inquisition,

telling me with Surrey loam caked
on the tongue, home is always elsewhere.
I take it like an English middleweight
with a questionable chin, knowing

my passport photo's too open-faced,
haircut wrong (an afro) for the decade;
the stamp, British Citizen not bold enough
for my liking and too much for theirs.

The cockney cab driver begins chirpily
but can't or won't steer clear of race,
so rounds on Asians. I lock eyes with him
in the rearview when I say I live with one.

He settles at the wheel grudgingly,
in a huffed silence. Cha! Drive man!
I have legal tender burning in my pocket
to move on, like a cross in Transylvania.

At my front door, why doesn't the lock
recognize me and budge? I give an extra
twist and fall forward over the threshold
piled with the felicitations of junk mail,

into a cool reception in the hall.
Grey light and close skies I love you.
Chokey streets, roundabouts and streetlamps
with tyres chucked round them, I love you.

Police officer, your boots need re-heeling.
Robin Redbreast, special request—a burst
of song so the worm can wind to the surface.
We must all sing for our suppers or else.

Peter Didsbury was born in 1946 in Fleetwood, Lancashire, and works as an archae-ologist. Didsbury is another gravely underrated talent; his wit is often so dry some might read him straight, so quick too many miss it. Didsbury's work also has an imagist and symbolist streak that reveals its deep kinship with European poetry. He often seems a kind of archivist of daily astonishments, writing about the contemporary as if it were already another classical or golden age, and has the true poet's knack (one with which so many are so often undeservedly credited) of rendering the quotidian detail in a miraculous light, the light of its own freakish singularity.

FURTHER READING:
That Old-Time Religion (Bloodaxe, 1994), *The Classical Farm* (Bloodaxe, 1987)

The Shorter Life

I loved the rain,
but always suffered badly
from post-pluvial *tristesse.*

My best wet afternoon was in the mouth
of a disused railway tunnel,
behind me the mile-long carbon-encrusted dark.

That Old-Time Religion

God and His angels stroll in the garden
before turning in for the night.
They've adopted the style
of rich and gifted young Englishmen this evening
and also, bizarrely even for them, decided that they'll speak
in nothing but Sumerian to each other
which all are agreed was a truly heavenly language.

It isn't long before God starts boasting,
in Sumerian of course, that He's the only Being He knows
who knows by heart *The Bothie of Tober-na-Vuolich*,
and is about to prove it when Lucifer intercedes
to make the points that

    a) they've all agreed to speak Sumerian, which was never the
       tongue of that estimable poem, and that unless He wants to
       pay the usual forfeit, which wouldn't really be consonant
       with His divinity, He'd better give up the idea;

    b) should He decide to do it into
       instantaneous and perfect Sumerian metres,
       a feat of which they're all aware He's capable,
       He wouldn't be proving His grasp of the original
       and would run the risk of them thinking Him a show-off;

  & c) since He, God, and not Arthur Hugh Clough must be regarded
       as the only true author of *The Bothie*, as of all things,
       he, Satan, doesn't see what the point of it would be anyway.

In the silence which follows the Creator is keenly aware
of the voice of the nightingale, then murmurs of consensus,
then much delighted laughter from the angels.

Lucifer bows.

The nightingale stops singing.

God sighs. He could really do without these bitches sometimes
but *then* where would He be?

As if to answer this question to Himself
He withdraws to the farthest reaches of the garden
and leans on the parapet, smoking in fitful gloom,
for what seems like an eternity.

He lights each gasper from the butt of His last
then flicks the glowing end far into the dark,
displeased at His foreknowledge of where it will fall.
To KNOW what His more intelligent creatures have thought
of these lights that appear in August out of Perseus
and not to have disabused them of it, as He's always meant to,
is unforgivable. He gazes in their direction in the dark
and gives them His Word that soon He will change all that,
silent at first, then whispered, then *shouted* in Sumerian.

Part of the Bridge

(for Robin Moore)

The enormous mentality
of the south bank abutment's
embedded concrete block
is not impassive,
though it copes with the westering sun
as remorselessly as any god with petitions.

It is not to be blamed for its size,
its faces textured with jutting tablets, grooves,
or even our dear conviction that mass,
when sheer enough, moves over into sentience.

To enter its zone on an evening in July
is to speak the word *temple*
in as emptiness-sanctioned a voice
as is used among the mountains;

to hear what it does with the fabulations of air,
that move in its precinct like spirits of ancient birds,
is to know both the paradox, and the stimulus, of its pity.

Chandlery

Here is your wooden keg.

It contains your astrolabe,
carefully packed in oysters.

I could do you black powder
if you cared to change your mind.

Or from perfect darkness a tethered animal,
one that would give you some milk.

❧ MICHAEL DONAGHY

Michael Donaghy was born in New York in 1954. He has lived in London since 1985, where he works as a teacher and musician. Donaghy's poems have deservedly won praise for their elegance and compression, though some critics have missed their frequent deployment of very dark humour and Borgesian paradox. In their flawless technique, they seem, perhaps, built to last in a way few other poets in the language can currently rival. Donaghy often writes poems of apparent lightness, but great philosophical, argumentative and allusive density. He obsesses over memory and its fictions, and the problems of faith.

FURTHER READING:
Dances Learned Last Night—Poems 1975–1995 (Picador, 2000), *Conjure* (Picador, 2000)

Machines

Dearest, note how these two are alike:
This harpsichord pavane by Purcell
And the racer's twelve-speed bike.

The machinery of grace is always simple.
This chrome trapezoid, one wheel connected
To another of concentric gears,
Which Ptolemy dreamt of and Schwinn perfected,
Is gone. The cyclist, not the cycle, steers.
And in the playing, Purcell's chords are played away.

So this talk, or touch if I were there,
Should work its effortless gadgetry of love,
Like Dante's heaven, and melt into the air.

If it doesn't, of course, I've fallen. So much is chance,
So much agility, desire, and feverish care,
As bicyclists and harpsichordists prove

Who only by moving can balance,
Only by balancing move.

Shibboleth

One didn't know the name of Tarzan's monkey.
Another couldn't strip the cellophane
From a GI's pack of cigarettes.
By such minutiae were the infiltrators detected.

By the second week of battle
We'd become obsessed with trivia.
At a sentry point, at midnight, in the rain,
An ignorance of baseball could be lethal.

The morning of the first snowfall, I was shaving,
Staring into a mirror nailed to a tree,
Intoning the Christian names of the Andrews Sisters.
'Maxine, Laverne, Patty.'

The Bacchae

Look out, Slim, these girls are trouble.
You dance with them they dance you back.
They talk it broad but they want it subtle
and you got too much mouth for that.
Their secret groove's their sacred grove—
not clever not ever, nor loud, nor flaunt.
I know you, Slim, you're a jerk for love.
The way you talk is the what you want.
You want numbers. You want names.

You want to cheat at rouge et noir.
But these are initiated dames—
the how they move is the what they are.

Caliban's Books

Hair oil, boiled sweets, chalk dust, squid's ink . . .
Bear with me. I'm trying to conjure my father,
age fourteen, as Caliban—picked by Mr Quinn
for the role he was born to play because
'I was the handsomest boy at school'
he'll say, straight-faced, at fifty.
This isn't easy. I've only half the spell,
and I won't be born for twenty years.
I'm trying for rainlight on Belfast Lough
and listening for a small, blunt accent
barking over the hiss of a stove getting louder like surf.
But how can I read when the schoolroom's gone
black as the hold of a ship? Start again.

Hair oil, boiled sweets . . .
But his paperbacks are crumbling in my hands,
seachanged bouquets, each brown page
scribbled on, underlined, memorized,
forgotten like used pornography:
The Pocket Treasury of English Verse,
How to Win Friends and Influence People,
Thirty Days to a More Powerful Vocabulary.

Fish stink, pitch stink, seaspray, cedarwood . . .
I seem to have brought us to the port of Naples,
midnight, to a shadow below deck
dreaming of a distant island.
So many years, so many ports ago!

The moment comes. It slips from the hold
and knucklewalks across the dark piazza
sobbing *maestro! maestro!* But the duke's long dead
and all his magic books are drowned.

A Repertoire

'Play us one we've never heard before'
we'd ask this old guy in our neighbourhood.
He'd rosin up a good three or four
seconds, stalling, but he always could.
This was the Bronx in 1971,
when every night the sky was pink with arson.
He ran a bar beneath the el, the Blarney Stone,
and there one Easter day he sat us down
and made us tape as much as he could play;
'I gave you these. Make sure you put that down',
meaning all he didn't have to say.

All that summer we slept on fire escapes,
or tried to sleep, while sirens or the brass
from our neighbour's Tito Puente tapes
kept us up and made us late for mass.
I found our back door bent back to admit
beneath the thick sweet reek of grass
a nest of needles, bottlecaps, and shit.
By August Tom had sold the Blarney Stone
to Puerto Ricans, paid his debts in cash
but left enough to fly his body home.

The bar still rises from the South Bronx ash,
its yellow neon buzzing in the noonday
dark beneath the el, a sheet-steel door
bolted where he played each second Sunday.

'Play me one I've never heard before'
I'd say, and whether he recalled those notes
or made them up, or—since it was Tom who played—
whether it was something in his blood
(cancer, and he was childless and afraid)
I couldn't tell you. And he always would.

᧘ CAROL ANN DUFFY

Carol Ann Duffy was born in 1955 in Glasgow, Scotland, and grew up in Stafford, England. She now lives in Manchester. Duffy is the most popular poet in the UK, and perhaps the only poet besides Simon Armitage to have gained such a wide readership and still enjoy the respect and admiration of her peers. Duffy's simultaneously accessible and dense poetry is a small miracle of stylistic balance, and a hugely influential model for many younger poets. Her witty and often powerfully subversive feminist reimaginings of myth and history have, however, been perhaps too widely imitated; these strategies are nothing without Duffy's immense flair for the dramatic monologue, and eye and ear for the surreal.

FURTHER READING:
Selected Poems (Penguin, 1994), *The World's Wife* (Faber & Faber, 1999)

Prayer

Some days, although we cannot pray, a prayer
utters itself. So, a woman will lift
her head from the sieve of her hands and stare
at the minims sung by a tree, a sudden gift.

Some nights, although we are faithless, the truth
enters our hearts, that small familiar pain;
then a man will stand stock-still, hearing his youth
in the distant Latin chanting of a train.

Pray for us now. Grade I piano scales
console the lodger looking out across
a Midlands town. Then dusk, and someone calls
a child's name as though they named their loss.

Darkness outside. Inside, the radio's prayer—
Rockall. Malin. Dogger. Finisterre.

Warming Her Pearls

for Judith Radstone

Next to my own skin, her pearls. My mistress
bids me wear them, warm them, until evening
when I'll brush her hair. At six, I place them
round her cool, white throat. All day I think of her,

resting in the Yellow Room, contemplating silk
or taffeta, which gown tonight? She fans herself
whilst I work willingly, my slow heat entering
each pearl. Slack on my neck, her rope.

She's beautiful. I dream about her
in my attic bed; picture her dancing
with tall men, puzzled by my faint, persistent scent
beneath her French perfume, her milky stories.

I dust her shoulders with a rabbit's foot,
watch the soft blush seep through her skin
like an indolent sigh. In her looking-glass
my red lips part as though I want to speak.

Full moon. Her carriage brings her home. I see
her every movement in my head . . . Undressing,
taking off her jewels, her slim hand reaching
for the case, slipping naked into bed, the way

she always does . . . And I lie here awake,
knowing the pearls are cooling even now
in the room where my mistress sleeps. All night
I feel their absence and I burn.

Little Red-Cap

At childhood's end, the houses petered out
into playing fields, the factory, allotments
kept, like mistresses, by kneeling married men,
the silent railway line, the hermit's caravan,
till you came at last to the edge of the woods.
It was there that I first clapped eyes on the wolf.

He stood in a clearing, reading his verse out loud
in his wolfy drawl, a paperback in his hairy paw,
red wine staining his bearded jaw. What big ears
he had! What big eyes he had! What teeth!
In the interval, I made quite sure he spotted me,
sweet sixteen, never been, babe, waif, and bought me a drink,

my first. You might ask why. Here's why. Poetry.
The wolf, I knew, would lead me deep into the woods,
away from home, to a dark tangled thorny place
lit by the eyes of owls. I crawled in his wake,
my stockings ripped to shreds, scraps of red from my blazer
snagged on twig and branch, murder clues. I lost both shoes

but got there, wolf's lair, better beware. Lesson one that night,
breath of the wolf in my ear, was the love poem.
I clung till dawn to his thrashing fur, for
what little girl doesn't dearly love a wolf?
Then I slid from between his heavy matted paws
and went in search of a living bird—white dove—

which flew, straight, from my hands to his open mouth.
One bite, dead. How nice, breakfast in bed, he said,
licking his chops. As soon as he slept, I crept to the back
of the lair, where a whole wall was crimson, gold, aglow
    with books.

Words, words were truly alive on the tongue, in the head,
warm, beating, frantic, winged; music and blood.

But then I was young—and it took ten years
in the woods to tell that a mushroom
stoppers the mouth of a buried corpse, that birds
are the uttered thought of trees, that a greying wolf
howls the same old song at the moon, year in, year out,
season after season, same rhyme, same reason. I took an axe

to a willow to see how it wept. I took an axe to a salmon
to see how it leapt. I took an axe to the wolf
as he slept, one chop, scrotum to throat, and saw
the glistening, virgin white of my grandmother's bones.
I filled his old belly with stones. I stitched him up.
Out of the forest I come with my flowers, singing, all alone.

Circe

I'm fond, nereids and nymphs, unlike some, of the pig,
of the tusker, the snout, the boar and the swine.
One way or another, all pigs have been mine—
under my thumb, the bristling, salty skin of their backs,
in my nostrils here, their yobby, porky colognes.
I'm familiar with hogs and runts, their percussion of oinks
and grunts, their squeals. I've stood with a pail of swill
at dusk, at the creaky gate of the sty,
tasting the sweaty, spicy air, the moon
like a lemon popped in the mouth of the sky.
But I want to begin with a recipe from abroad

which uses the cheek—and the tongue in cheek
at that. Lay two pig's cheeks, with the tongue,
in a dish, and strew it well over with salt

and cloves. Remember the skills of the tongue—
to lick, to lap, to loosen, lubricate, to lie
in the soft pouch of the face—and how each pig's face
was uniquely itself, as many handsome as plain,
the cowardly face, the brave, the comical, noble,
sly or wise, the cruel, the kind, but all of them,
nymphs, with those piggy eyes. Season with mace.

Well-cleaned pig's ears should be blanched, singed, tossed
in a pot, boiled, kept hot, scraped, served, garnished
with thyme. Look at that simmering lug, at that ear,
did it listen, ever, to you, to your prayers and rhymes,
to the chimes of your voice, singing and clear? Mash
the potatoes, nymph, open the beer. Now to the brains,
to the trotters, shoulders, chops, to the sweetmeats slipped
from the slit, bulging, vulnerable bag of the balls.
When the heart of a pig has hardened, dice it small.

Dice it small. I, too, once knelt on this shining shore
watching the tall ships sail from the burning sun
like myths; slipped off my dress to wade,
breast-deep, in the sea, waving and calling;
then plunged, then swam on my back, looking up
as three black ships sighed in the shallow waves.
Of course, I was younger then. And hoping for men. Now,
let us baste that sizzling pig on the spit once again.

Ian Duhig was born in London in 1954 of Irish parents and now lives in Leeds. Duhig's marvellous tales are scholarly, ludic, and often extremely funny. Some read like scriptorium marginalia, both learned and profane—but Duhig is also a master balladeer and engages directly with a folk tradition in a very sophisticated way, like the older Charles Causley, that wholly succeeds in honouring it without patronising it. Duhig's concern with social history is perhaps the deepest of the poets presented here; he seems committed to an almost folk ideal that poetry is still the best way to commemorate our lives, loves, and work.

FURTHER READING:
The Bradford Count (Bloodaxe, 1991), *The Lammas Hireling* (Picador, 2003)

Fundamentals

Brethren, I know that many of you have come here today
because your Chief has promised any non-attender
that he will stake him out, drive tent-pegs through his anus
and sell his wives and children to the Portuguese.
As far as possible, I want you to put that from your minds.
Today, I want to talk to you about the Christian God.

In many respects, our Christian God is not like your God.
His name, for example, is not also our word for rain.
Neither does it have for us the connotation 'sexual intercourse'.
And although I call Him 'holy' (we call Him 'Him', not 'It',
even though we know He is not a man and certainly not a woman)
I do not mean, as you do, that He is fat like a healthy cow.

Let me make this clear. When I say 'God is good, God is everywhere',
it is not because He is exceptionally fat. 'God loves you'
does not mean what warriors do to spear-carriers on campaign.
It means He feels for you like your mother or your father—
yes I know Chuma loved a son he bought like warriors
love spear-carriers on campaign—that's *Sin* and it comes later.

From today, I want you to remember just three simple things:
our God is different from your God, our God is better than your God
and my wife doesn't like it when you watch her go to the toilet.
Grasp them and you have grasped the fundamentals of salvation.
Baptisms start at sundown but before then, as arranged,
how to strip, clean and re-sight a bolt-action Martini-Henry.

Chocolate Soldier

(Air: 'The Kerry Recruit')

To Rowntrees one morning
    down Walmgate I strolled
handsome as Samson
    and doubly bold
when up poles this Sergeant
    who'd have me enlist—
gives me the handshake
    the bob in his fist.

I said keep your bob,
    get drink or a dance—
I'm sure to enlist
    with a war on in France;
but he showed me the make
    of his recruiting stick
and I woke with a headache
    in damned Catterick.

They forced me to wear
    this stiff uniform
and Jesus that summer
    got warmer than warm;

they gave me a badge
    they gave me a gun
and told me I'd frighten
    the shite from The Hun.

Troops in a fortnight,
    we lined a Hull quay
to board a tin warship
    for High Germany;
I thought of my girl
    when I touched the hard tin,
and I tell you I missed
    the kind warmth of her skin.

We tramped up the line
    for hundreds of miles
both cold, wet and hungry
    I'd wonderful piles;
next morning for action
    our Sarge gives a yell;
we ate a hot breakfast
    of shrapnel and shell.

After the first charge
    morale was quite sound;
both heads, legs and arms
    lay scattered around.
I looked at my pals
    then wished I had died;
the rest of the war
    I took in my stride.

Shipped back to Yorkshire
    with gongs but no pay,
we found out that Rowntrees
    gave our jobs away.

My girl palmed me off
   with style and with grace;
I met my old Sarge
   and I spat in his face.

He owned he deserved it
   for strokes by and by—
it wasn't the first time
   I'd wiped Sarge's eye;
then he mentioned work
   in Old Ireland
I looked in his eye
   and I spat on my hand.

I hated my last kit
   but cursed this one worse;
a collar so tight
   they'd to send for the nurse
and jacket and trousers
   more fit for a clown,
with one of them black
   and the other one brown.

Well Ireland was good
   if rebels are bad—
you'd never believe
   all the girls that we had;
through fire and through flood
   we'd fight and not yield
and sometimes we tret them
   like beasts of the field.

We ambushed near Cashel
   this hard Shinner get;
I gelded the bastard
   with my bayonet

but what's past is past,
　　let's live and let live,
forgive and forget
　　and forget and forgive.

My new uniform
　　is Vincent de Paul's;
I look like a cunt
　　but it warms the old balls.
I know life's all luck
　　and love a bad joke
I don't drink too much
　　'cause I haven't the poke.

But I mustn't grumble
　　'cause I do OK;
the world and old Walmgate
　　are colder today—
so all you young squaddies
　　God save you from hurt;
ask my advice
　　and I'll tell you desert.

The Lammas Hireling

for Robert Walters

After the fair, I'd still a light heart
And a heavy purse, he struck so cheap.
And cattle doted on him: in his time,
Mine only dropped heifers, fat as cream.
Yields doubled. I grew fond of company
That knew when to shut up. The one night,

Disturbed from dreams of my dear late wife,
I hunted down her torn voice to his pale form.
Stock-still in the light from the dark lantern,
Stark naked but for the fox-trap biting his ankle,
I knew him a warlock, a cow with leather horns.
To go into the hare gets you muckle sorrow,

The wisdom runs, muckle care. I levelled
And blew the small hour through his heart.
The moon came out. By its yellow witness
I saw him fur over like a stone mossing.
His lovely head thinned. His top lip gathered.
His eyes rose like bread. I carried him

In a sack that grew lighter at every step
And dropped him from a bridge. There was no
Splash. Now my herd's elf-shot. I don't dream
But spend my nights casting ball from half-crowns
And my days here. Bless me Father I have sinned.
It has been an hour since my last confession.

✑ PAUL FARLEY

Paul Farley was born in Liverpool in 1965 and now teaches at Lancaster University. As a non-metropolitan male poet, Farley has occasionally been compared (mainly by critics reduced to forcing connections between the five things they have actually read) to Simon Armitage, though Farley's debts are to the Ulster poet Derek Mahon, and—like Michael Donaghy—the Richard Wilbur of discursive masterpieces such as 'The Mind-Reader' and 'Walking to Sleep'; he has also been influenced by his study of the visual arts. Farley's imagination is often prompted by things, from which he will develop labyrinths of association and memory. Like O'Brien and Didsbury, he is a kind of archivist of the present; his poems often seem set in a kind of contemporary Pompeii.

FURTHER READING:
The Boy From the Chemist Is Here to See You (Picador, 1998), *Ice Age* (Picador, 2002)

Treacle

Funny to think you can still buy it now,
a throwback, like shoe polish or the sardine key.
When you lever the lid it opens with a sigh
and you're face-to-face with history.
By that I mean the unstable pitch black
you're careful not to spill, like mercury

that doesn't give any reflection back,
that gets between the cracks of everything
and holds together the sandstone and bricks
of our museums and art galleries;
and though those selfsame buildings stand
hosed clean now of all their gunk and soot,

feel the weight of this tin in your hand,
read its endorsement from one Abram Lyle
'Out of the strong came forth sweetness'

below the weird logo of bees in swarm
like a halo over the lion carcass.
Breathe its scent, something lost from our streets

like horseshit or coalsmoke; its base note
a building block as biblical as honey,
the last dregs of an empire's dark sump;
see how a spoonful won't let go of its past,
what the tin calls back to the mean of its lip
as you pour its contents over yourself

and smear it into every orifice.
You're history now, a captive explorer
staked out for the insects; you're tarred
and feel its caul harden. The restorer
will tap your details back out of the dark:
close-in work with a toffee hammer.

The Lamp

(At sea, Dec 29, 1849)

Aboard, at home again, this book closes.
No written record of that westbound voyage
survives. I have you travelling with the sun
and mangy Irish packets, dreaming up
your story. Five weeks berthed alone, below
the waterline, immersed in printed matter
from Holborn, Charing Cross Road, and the Strand.
Was it like this? The artificial glow
of sperm oil lit those words across the miles
of ocean swells. Having the presence of mind,
you saw yourself, a reader in the dark,
dependant on the whale's 'sweet grass butter'.

The lamp hung true despite the pitch and roll.
You had the shortest chapter by landfall.

Diary Moon

You are the plainest moon. Forget all others:
shivering in pools, or spoken to when drunk,
that great Romantic gaze of youth; shed all
sonatas, harvests, Junes, and think instead
of how your phases turn here in a diary:
stripped of sunlight, surface noise and seas
you move unnoticed through the months, a bare limn
achieving ink blackness, emptying again.

You who turned inside the week-to-view
my father carried round each year, past crosses
that symbolized pay days, final demands;
in girlfriends', where red novae marked the dates
they were 'due on', and I shouldn't've been looking;
who even showed in weighty Filofaxes,
peeping through the clouds of missed appointments,
arrivals and departures, names and numbers.

On nights like these, which of us needs reminding
to set an eel-trap, open up the bomb doors
or sail out of the harbour on a spring-tide?
What sway do you hold over our affairs?
Although for some you're all that's there, printed
across the white weeks until New Year;
moving towards windows that will not frame us,
into the evenings of our sons and daughters.

An Interior

They ask why I still bother coming back.
London must be great this time of year.
I'm not listening. My eyes have found
the draining-board, its dull mineral shine,
the spice rack, still exactly how I left it,
knives, a Vermeer vinyl table-mat.
How many hours did I spend watching
the woman pouring milk into a bowl
that never fills? I never tired of it.
Vision persists, doesn't admit the breaks
the artist must have taken, leg-stretching
alongside a canal twitching with sky
not unlike the leaden one outside;
or just leant on the door jamb, looking out
onto a courtyard, smoking a pipe
before going in, to sleep on his excitement.

Peter and the Dyke

He's in there still, with Johnny Appleseed,
with all the frogs and sleeping princesses
but won't budge. I've tempted him with liquorice,
with pipe tobacco and Dutch magazines.
This is dedication, a child's endurance.
Outside, the longshore drift of my late teens
and pull of every tide that's turned since
are as nothing to his freezing fingertip.

∽ JAMES FENTON

James Fenton was born in Lincoln, England, in 1949; he has worked as a drama critic, foreign correspondent, and a gardening columnist. It's a great regret to many of us that Fenton has not devoted himself more seriously to the art. When he has turned his hand to more than improvisations and song-lyrics, the results have a rare and breathtaking lightness, balance, and strength, like something built for man-powered flight. Fenton is perhaps too inhibited by his deep appreciation of the masters (his book of essays, *The Strength of Poetry*, was the most significant—and certainly the most exquisitely written—volume of criticism to have appeared in the UK in the last thirty years); however he has also written a handful of poems which are among the finest—and perhaps, ultimately, the most characteristic—-of the age.

SUGGESTED READING:
The Memory of War/Children in Exile: Poems 1968–83 (Salamander Press/ Penguin, 1992)

Wind

This is the wind, the wind in a field of corn.
Great crowds are fleeing from a major disaster
Down the long valleys, the green swaying wadis,
Down through the beautiful catastrophe of wind.

Families, tribes, nations and their livestock
Have heard something, seen something. An expectation
Or a gigantic misunderstanding has swept over the hilltop
Bending the ear of the hedgerow with stories of fire and sword.

I saw a thousand years pass in two seconds.
Land was lost, languages rose and divided.
This lord went east and found safety.
His brother sought Africa and a dish of aloes.

Centuries, minutes later, one might ask
How the hilt of a sword wandered so far from the smithy.

And somewhere they will sing: 'Like chaff we were borne
In the wind.' This is the wind in a field of corn.

A Staffordshire Murderer

Every fear is a desire. Every desire is fear.
The cigarettes are burning under the trees
Where the Staffordshire murderers wait for their accomplices
And victims. Every victim is an accomplice.

It takes a lifetime to stroll to the carpark
Stopping at the footbridge for reassurance,
Looking down at the stream, observing
(With one eye) the mallard's diagonal progress backwards.

You could cut and run, now. It is not too late.
But your fear is like a long-case clock
In the last whirring second before the hour,
The hammer drawn back, the heart ready to chime.

Fear turns the ignition. The van is unlocked.
You may learn now what you ought to know:
That every journey begins with a death,
That the suicide travels alone, that the murderer needs company.

And the Staffordshire murderers, nervous though they are,
Are masters of the conciliatory smile.
A cigarette? A tablet in a tin?
Would you care for a boiled sweet from the famous poisoner

Of Rugeley? These are his own brand.
He has never had any complaints.
He speaks of his victims as a sexual braggart
With a tradesman's emphasis on the word 'satisfaction'.

You are flattered as never before. He appreciates
So much, the little things—your willingness for instance
To bequeath your body at once to his experiments.
He sees the point of you as no one else does.

Large parts of Staffordshire have been undermined.
The trees are in it up to their necks. Fish
Nest in their branches. In one of the Five Towns
An ornamental pond disappeared overnight

Dragging the ducks down with it, down to the old seams
With a sound as of a gigantic bath running out,
Which is in turn the sound of ducks in distress.
Thus History murders mallards, while we hear nothing

Or what we hear we do not understand.
It is heard as the tramp's rage in the crowded precinct:
'Woe to the bloody city of Lichfield'.
It is lost in the enthusiasm of the windows

From which we are offered on the easiest terms
Five times over in colour and once in monochrome
The first reprisals after the drill-sergeant's coup.
How speedily the murder detail makes its way

Along the green beach, past the pink breakers,
And binds the whole cabinet to the oildrums,
Where death is a preoccupied tossing of the head,
Where no decorative cloud lingers at the gun's mouth.

At the Dame's School dust gathers on the highwayman,
On Sankey and Moody, Wesley and Fox,
On the snoring churchwarden, on Palmer the Poisoner
And Palmer's house and Stanfield Hall.

The brilliant moss has been chipped from the Red Barn.
They say that Cromwell played ping-pong with the cathedral.
We train roses over the arches. In the Minster Pool
Crayfish live under carved stones. Every spring

The rats pick off the young mallards and
The good weather brings out the murderers
By the Floral Clock, by the footbridge,
The pottery murderers in jackets of prussian blue.

'Alack, George, where are thy shoes?'
He lifted up his head and espied the three
Steeple-house spires, and they struck at his life.
And he went by his eye over hedge and ditch

And no one laid hands on him, and he went
Thus crying through the streets, where there seemed
To be a channel of blood running through the streets,
And the market-place appeared like a pool of blood.

For this field of corpses was Lichfield
Where a thousand Christian Britons fell
In Diocletian's day, and 'much could I write
Of the sense that I had of the blood—'

That winter Friday. Today it is hot.
The cowparsley is so high that the van cannot be seen
From the road. The bubbles rise in the warm canal.
Below the lock-gates you can hear mallards.

A coot hurries along the tow-path, like a Queen's Messenger.
On the heli-pad, an arrival in blue livery
Sends the water-boatmen off on urgent business.
News of a defeat. Keep calm. The cathedral chimes.

The house by the bridge is the house in your dream.
It stares through new frames, unwonted spectacles,
And the paint, you can tell, has been weeping.
In the yard, five striped oildrums. Flowers in a tyre.

This is where the murderer works. But it is Sunday.
Tomorrow's bank holiday will allow the bricks to set.
You see? he has thought of everything. He shows you
The snug little cavity he calls 'your future home'.

And 'Do you know,' he remarks, 'I have been counting my victims.
Nine hundred and ninety-nine, the Number of the Beast!
That makes you . . .' But he sees he has overstepped the mark:
I'm sorry, but you cannot seriously have thought you were the first?'

A thousand preachers, a thousand poisoners,
A thousand martyrs, a thousand murderers—
Surely these preachers are poisoners, these martyrs murderers?
Surely this is all a gigantic mistake?

But there has been no mistake. God and the weather are glorious.
You have come as an anchorite to kneel at your funeral.
Kneel then and pray. The blade flashes a smile.
This is your new life. This murder is yours.

In a Notebook

There was a river overhung with trees
With wooden houses built along its shallows
From which the morning sun drew up a haze
And the gyrations of the early swallows
Paid no attention to the gentle breeze
Which spoke discreetly from the weeping willows.
There was a jetty by the forest clearing
Where a small boat was tugging at its mooring.

And night still lingered underneath the eaves.
In the dark houseboats families were stirring
And Chinese soup was cooked on charcoal stoves.
Then one by one there came into the clearing
Mothers and daughters bowed beneath their sheaves.
The silent children gathered round me staring
And the shy soldiers setting out for battle
Asked for a cigarette and laughed a little.

From low canoes old men laid out their nets
While on the bank young boys with lines were fishing.
The wicker traps were drawn up by their floats.
The girls stood waist-deep in the river washing
Or tossed the day's rice on enamel plates
And I sat drinking bitter coffee wishing
The tide would turn to bring me to my senses
After the pleasant war and the evasive answers.

There was a river overhung with trees.
The girls stood waist-deep in the river washing,
And night still lingered underneath the eaves
While on the bank young boys with lines were fishing.
Mothers and daughters bowed beneath their sheaves
While I sat drinking bitter coffee wishing—
And the tide turned and brought me to my senses.
The pleasant war brought the unpleasant answers.

The villages are burnt, the cities void;
The morning light has left the river view;
The distant followers have been dismayed;
And I'm afraid, reading this passage now,
That everything I knew has been destroyed
By those whom I admired but never knew;
The laughing soldiers fought to their defeat
And I'm afraid most of my friends are dead.

ℳ MARK FORD

Mark Ford was born in Nairobi, Kenya, in 1962 and lives in London. Ford wouldn't be the writer he is without the those imaginative freedoms won by the New York School, and O'Hara and Ashbery in particular—his poems display much of Ashbery's studied offhandedness and dramatic shifts of register—and yet Ford's remains a very English take on things. For all the improvisatory flair, these are tightly constructed compositions of considerable complexity. Ford's work is also of its time, in the best possible sense, and he has the knack of casting the contemporary in almost an historic light.

FURTHER READING:
Landlocked (Chatto & Windus, 1992), *Soft Sift* (Faber & Faber, 2001)

Looping the Loop

Anything can be forgotten, become regular
As newspapers hurled in a spinning arc to land
With a thump on the porch where Grandma sits
And knits, her hound dog yawning at her feet.

And other strangled details will emerge and prove
Suddenly potent to confound the wary-footed, and even
The assembled members of the panel; in turn
Each pundit speaks, yanks from the hat an angry rabbit who flops

In spurts around the circular paths of crazy paving.
No pressing need to watch them but you do.

ℳ

Dirty fingernails in August, and just
The amount of lightning threatened; superb
Courtiers sweep through the various precincts
Fingering each other's beads in the jagged dusk.

I myself went and left like a moron, but heard
The rumours nonetheless—meanwhile the wind
Pounds this shack with wilful abandon, then inquires,
As it eases, just exactly how many spliffs there were

Stashed that night in the cicada-coloured
Pencil case tucked in the side pocket of her satchel.

        ⌒

Harsh truths indeed! I act the part of my own
Nemesis, polite, dazed, addicted to adversity,
Frequently drunk. Overhead the wires hum
Obscure ultimatums, mutterings that threaten

To aggravate forever these ordinary feelings, and inflict
Upon the world quantities of crazily-worded postcards
Sent off on impulse from decaying seaside towns. For I still
Love the tang of brine, the old women hurtling on motorbikes

Through swirling banks of fog, any who loiter
Resentfully about the war memorial on summer afternoons.

        ⌒

Eventually one hears the cuckoo's call, while friends
Recline in armchairs. Let's off then, backwards through
The fish-eye lens, bone by bone, clean shirts
Soon streaked and torn. Some fought like lovers

Under the bluish lights that swayed so weirdly
On their stanchions of pale, unpainted metal; how
Suddenly the team began to perform as if a stranger
Watched and cared, blindly probing through the endless rain

For openings, reeling back aghast, bitterly dispersed
One dank October, the sediment settling as best it might.

&

Afloat on the flood, indifferent to the cries
And the silence, I imprison your wandering hand:
In it lurk anecdote and polemic entwined, scars
Faint as a plate's, the luck of the stars . . .

Yet the affect hardly emerges, peers forth
Like a strayed mole through a cliff-crevice
On the unfamiliar scene; though I have leapt and held
And carried, grimaced sourly at the brimming heavens,

A few feints and the incident spirals
Beyond reach, turns turtle in dreams displaced before morning.

The Long Man

of Wilmington winces with the dawn; he has just
endured yet another mythical, pointless, starry
vigil. His ankles ache, and the weather looks
irksome and moody; the early traffic whizzes by
regardless, but the news and emblems borne
by each car permeate the soil that sustains
the straggling furze, various grasses, and the odd
towering oak. Across the damp fields a distant
siren pleads for attention; he cannot
move, nor, like a martyr, disprove the lie of the land.

Who was it who established, in the teeth
of so much evidence, the laws of diminishing
returns? I woke up feeling cold and distended,

my feet pointing east, my head in low-hanging
clouds. A stream of curious tags and sayings
flowed like a potion through my veins. I had
the 'look', as some called it, meaning I floated
in an envelope of air that ducked and sheered
between invisible obstacles. The alarmed
senses struggled to respond, then bewailed
the absence of detailed, all-powerful
precedents: I kept picturing someone tracing
a figure on the turf, and wearing this outline
into a path by walking and walking around
the hollow head, immobile limbs, and cavernous torso.

Early to Bed, Early to Rise

It was in Berlin you mixed up John and J. J. Cale,
And we found ourselves watching Jacques Tourneur's *Out of the
    Past* yet again.

I, on the other hand, confused Teniers the elder and Teniers the
    younger
In Amsterdam, where I saw Terry Gilliam's *Twelve Monkeys* on
    my own.

On the outskirts of Moscow we failed to distinguish clearly
    between Charles and Burl Ives;
Our punishment was to sit through Sergei Eisenstein's *Ivan the
    Terrible*, Parts I and II, twice.

I met a man in New York who couldn't tell the difference between
    George
And Zbigniew Herbert: his favourite film was Kenji Mizoguchi's
    Ugetsu Monogatari, which he insisted we see together.

In Cardiff I confounded Edward, Dylan, and R. S. Thomas;
To get over my embarrassment I went to a performance of Jean-Luc
    Godard's *Alphaville*.

People continually mistake the work of Antoine Le Nain for that of
    his brother Louis, even in Los Angeles,
Where most films are made, including Doug Liman's *Swingers*,
    which I recently saw for the first time, and really enjoyed.

⌀ JOHN GLENDAY

John Glenday was born in Monifeith, Scotland in 1952 and works as a drugs counsellor. Glenday is a kind of practical mystic and has been writing poems of quiet spiritual power for many years now, but is only starting to get the recognition he has almost studiously avoided. Glenday's subject is the soul and the soul of things. His work has a very un-British openness and clarity, reminiscent in tone perhaps only of the late Orcadian poet George Mackay Brown, though much closer in spirit to the shadows and transparencies of the Spanish and East European poetry he admires.

FURTHER READING:
The Apple Ghost (Peterloo, 1989), *Undark* (Peterloo, 1995)

Concerning the Atoms of the Soul

Someone explained once how the pieces of what we are
fall downwards at the same rate
as the Universe.
The atoms of us, falling towards the centre

of whatever everything is. And we don't see it.
We only sense their slight drag in the lifting hand.
That's what weight is, that communal process of falling.
Furthermore, those atoms carry hooks, like burrs,

hooks catching like hooks, like clinging to like,
that's what keeps us from becoming something else,
and why in early love, we sometimes
feel the tug of the heart snagging on another's heart.

Only the atoms of the soul are perfect spheres
with no means of holding on to the world
or perhaps no need for holding on,
and so they fall through our lives catching

against nothing, like perfect rain,
and in the end, he wrote, mix in that common well of light
at the centre of whatever the suspected
centre is, or might have been.

A Day at the Seaside

We're out in my father's boat and he's fishing.
He's fishing until the daylight goes.
It's the end of the season and I'm in the stern
to watch for the ebb that would pull us

out past the Buddon Light and the mouth of the river.
But I'm not watching the tide,
I'm watching him as he fishes, because I've never
seen him so focussed before—so engaged.

It's as if the fish had hooked him. Then just
as he makes his final cast, an oyster-catcher calls
far out across the water. Far out across
the water an oyster-catcher calls

just once, and then just once again, and then its silence calls.
The hurt lies not in the cross, but in the nails.

The Garden

for Erika

Just for a quarter of a day, I'd have you
follow me through the smoking willow herb

and my father's garden's half-seized gate, down
to that place where the knowledge of almost every-

thing comes undone in the powdery ceanothus shade;
where the apple goes withering back to blossom
in your palm, and the serpent, on its hind legs
in the shadows, leaves off whispering.

The Empire of Lights

After Magritte: L'Empire des Lumières 1954

The past is the antithesis of burglary. Imagine
a house in darkness. Or to be more precise,
imagine darkness in a house. Something akin

to that Magritte where the light is held
at tree's length by a clutch of tungsten bulbs.
The looming woods proofed with shadow thicker than tar.

In the House of the Past we move backwards
from room to room, forever closing doors
on ourselves, always closing doors.

In each room, we leave some of those little trinkets
we love most, that the house is stealing from us.
Because we cherish them, we abandon them

to the furniture of strangers. Whenever we go
the doors swing shut behind us without a sound,
and the dust drifts up into the ceiling like smoke.

Oh there is so much we would love to hold on to,
but so little room. If only we could come back,
if only we could come back in the morning,

things would be so much better. But on we must go,
creeping backwards through silent bedrooms,
closing doors quietly for fear of waking ourselves.

Emptying our pockets, emptying our hands. Heavy
with emptiness, we crouch down at last in the lee
of a shattered window, where we dream of those

ancient burdens, long resolved. And the fragments
of glass fidget like broken insects on the rug,
eager to heal where our fists will gently touch.

Hydrodamalis Gigas

after G W Steller

These beasts are four fathoms long, but perfectly gentle.
They roam the shallower waters like sea-cattle

and graze on the waving flags of kelp.
At the slightest wound their innards will flop

out with a great hissing sound,
but they haven't yet grown to fear mankind:

no matter how many of their number might be killed,
they never try to swim away—they are so mild.

When one is speared, its neighbours will rush in
and struggle to draw out the harpoon

with the blades of their little hooves.
They almost seem to have a grasp of what it is to love.

I once watched a bull return to its butchered
mate two days in a row, butting its flensed hide

and calling out quietly across the shingle till the darkness fell.
The flesh on the small calves tastes sweet as veal

and their fat is pleasantly coloured,
like the best Dutch butter.

The females are furnished with long, black teats.
Try brushing them with your fingertips

then note what happens next—even on the dead
they will grow firm and the sweet milk bleed.

∽ LAVINIA GREENLAW

Lavinia Greenlaw was born in London in 1963. Greenlaw's poetry manages an extremely productive tension between narrative drive and lyric brevity; her highly controlled (something occasionally, and wrongly, mistaken for coolness) and charged pieces often play their hand with an admirable deftness that leaves the reader with a conclusion that seems both inescapable and wholly surprising. Greenlaw takes a great interest in the human, and specifically in human conduct under pressure; the moral project is never far below the surface of her verse, and all the more powerful for its refusal of easy judgement. She is also a fine novelist.

FURTHER READING:
Night Photograph (Faber & Faber, 1994), *Minsk* (Faber & Faber, 2003)

Reading Akhmatova in Midwinter

The revelations of ice, exactly:
each leaf carries itself in glass,
each stem is a fuse in a transparent flex,

each blade, for once, truly metallic.
Trees on the hill explode like fireworks
for the minute the sun hits.

Fields hover: bleached sheets in the afternoon,
ghosts as the light goes.
The landscape shivers but holds.

Ice floes cruise the Delaware,
force it under in unnatural silence;
clarification I watch as I watch

the road—nothing but the grind of the plough
as it banks snow, drops salt and grit.
By dark these are just settled hills,

grains embedded in the new fall.
We, too, make little impression
walking back from town at midnight

on birds' feet—ducks' feet on the ramp
where we inch and scrabble our way to the door,
too numb to mind the slapstick.

How did you cross
those unlit, reinvented streets
with your fear of traffic and your broken shoe?

There are mornings when it drips and cracks.
We pull glass bars from railings,
chip at the car's shadow.

Three

Your shaved head on my thigh
evokes a third thing,
the quorum or casting vote of us

—as Aquinas struggled to fit
the perpetual quality of hair
into his logic of resurrection

so, wanting more for us,
you subtract another millimetre
from the setting of the razor's edge.

The Spirit of the Staircase

In our game of flight, half-way down
was as near mid-air as it got: a point
of no return we'd fling ourselves at
over and over, riding pillows or trays.
We were quick to smooth the edge
of each step, grinding the carpet
to glass on which we'd lose our grip.
The new stairs were our new toy,
the descent to an odd extension,
our four new rooms at flood level
in the sunken garden—a wing
dislocated from a hive. Young bees
with soft stripes and borderless nights,
we'd so far been squared away
in a twin-set of bunkbeds, so tight-knit,
my brother and I once woke up finishing
a conversation begun in a dream.
It had been the simplest exchange,
and one I'd give much to return to:
the greetings of shadows, unsurprised
at having met beneath the trees
and happy to set off again, alone,
back into the dark.

Zombies

1980, I was returned to the city exposed
in black and white as the lights went on and on.
A back-alley neon sign, the first I'd seen,
drew us sweetly down and in to brightness:
a doll's parasol, a spike of green cherries,

the physic of apricot brandy, actual limes
and morning-to-night shades of rum.
Newly old enough and government-moneyed,
we knocked them back, melting the ice
between us and the unaccustomed looseness
of being legitimate and free. What possessed us?
Was it the kick of spirits or the invisible syrup
in which they swam that worked in our veins,
charming us into a car and forty miles east

to the fields of our years of boredom?
Did we not remember the curse of this place?
How Sundays drank our blood as we watched
dry paint or the dust on the television screen.
How people died bursting out of a quiet life,
or from being written into a small world's stories.
Who can see such things and live to tell?
How we hunted all night for noise and love,
striking out once across ploughed and frozen earth,
lurching from rut to rut until at the edge
we smashed our way out through a hedge, to fall
eight feet to the road. Of course, we felt nothing.
Was it not ourselves who frightened us most?
As if brightness or sweetness could save us.

Electricity

The night you called to tell me
that the unevenness between the days
is as simple as meeting or not meeting,
I was thinking about electricity—
how at no point on a circuit
can power diminish or accumulate,

how you also need a lack of balance
for energy to be released. *Trust it.*
Once, being held like that,
no edge, no end and no beginning,
I could not tell our actions apart:
if it was you who lifted my head to the light,
if it was I who said how much I wanted
to look at your face. *Your beautiful face.*

✑ W. N. HERBERT

W. N. Herbert was born in Dundee in 1961 and now lives in North Shields, England. Herbert, a brilliant and notorious maverick, has been careful to ally himself with no school—not through mere political slipperiness, but a genuine wide-ranging and wholly indiscriminate interest in almost every literary movement. Herbert writes in both English and a kind of experimental 'plastic' Scots, and is also an energetic and compelling performer of his own work. The several poets called W. N. Herbert have collectively paid for this diversification, however, and he remains one of the most underrated of our leading poets. He is capable of everything from a kind of austere McDiarmidian neo-Modernism to the most outrageous comic excursions.

FURTHER READING:
Forked Tongue (Bloodaxe, 1994), *Cabaret McGonagall* (Bloodaxe, 1996)

Slow Animals Crossing

Lemurs somehow, at that lilt of the road
up and sideways at the trees, stooping through
the farmyard on the way to Derrybeg.
Surely there are slower creatures who could cross:
turtles with their solemn wiping gait
or sloths who swim as though to sink
is no disgrace, such aqualungs of air would be
trapped among their matted spider hair.
I think of water since that night was full of it
and white frogs leapt into my lights
like chewing gum attempting
to free itself from tarmac. And I think of lemurs
whenever I see that sign with its red letters
because of the night, and the story
of the three men walking home, and the man
on the left said 'goodnight' to someone, and
the man on the right, 'goodnight' to someone else
and the man in the middle asked who
were they talking to? And one had seen a man

and one had seen a woman, and both
described the third man's parents, turning off
at the road to the graveyard. And when I thought
of lemurs I'd forgotten they were named
for the Latin word for spirits, and I only saw,
crawling slowly in my mind across the night road
back to my parents' house and my daughter,
the bandit eyes and banded tails and soft grey backs
and the white hands of lemurs, delicately placed
upon the twist and the shrug of the road.

Cabaret McGonagall

Come as ye dottilt, brain-deid lunks,
ye hibernatin cyber-punks,
gadget-gadjies, comics-geeks,
guys wi perfick rat's physiques,
fowk wi fuck-aa social skills,
fowk that winnae tak thir pills:
gin ye cannae even pley fuitball
treh thi Cabaret McGonagall.

Thi decor pits a cap oan oorie,
ut's puke-n-flock a la Tandoori;
there's a sculpture made frae canine stools,
there's a robot armadillo drools
when shown a phone o thi Pope,
and a salad spinner cerved fae dope:
gin ye cannae design a piss oan thi mall
trek thi Cabaret McGonagall.

We got: Clangers, Blimpers, gowks in mohair jimpers,
Bangers, Whimpers, cats wi stupit simpers—
Ciamar a thu, how are you, and hoozit gaun pal,

welcome to thi Cabaret Guillaume McGonagall.
We got: Dadaists, badass gits, shits wi RADA voices,
Futurists wi sutured wrists and bygets o James Joyce's—
Bienvenue, wha thi fuck are you, let's drink thi nicht away,
come oan yir own, or oan thi phone, or to thi Cabaret.

Come as ye bards that cannae scan,
fowk too scared tae get a tan,
come as ye anxious-chicken tykes
wi stabilisers oan yir bikes,
fowk whas mithers waash thir pants,
fowk wha drink deodorants:
fowk that think they caused thi Fall
like thi Cabaret McGonagall.

Fur as that's cheesy, static, stale,
this place gaes sae faur aff thi scale
o ony Wigwam Bam-meter
mimesis wad brak thi pentameter;
in oarder tae improve thi species' genes,
t'e'll find self-oaperatin guillotines:
bring yir knittin, bring yir shawl
tae thi Cabaret McGonagall.

We got: Berkoffs, jerk-offs, noodles wi nae knickers,
Ubuists, tubes wi zits, poodles dressed as vicars—
Gutenaben Aiberdeen, wilkommen Cumbernauld,
thi dregs o Scoatlan gaither at Chez McGonagall.
We got: mimes in tights, a MacDiarmidite that'iz ainsel contradicts,
kelpies, selkies, grown men that think they're Picts—
Buonaserra Oban and Ola! tae as Strathsprey,
come in disguise fist tae despise thi haill damn Cabaret.

Panic-attack Mac is oor DJ,
thi drugs he tuke werr as Class A,
sae noo he cannae laive thi bog;

thon ambient soond's him layin a log.
Feelin hungry? sook a plook;
thi son o Sawney Bean's oor cook:
gin consumin humans diz not appal
treh thi Bistro de McGonagall.

Waatch Paranoia Pete pit speed
intil auld Flaubert's parrot's feed,
and noo ut's squaakin oot in leids
naebody kens till uts beak bleeds
and when ut faas richt aff uts perch,
Pete gees himsel a boady search:
thi evidence is there fur all
at thi Cabaret McGonagall.

We got: weirdos, beardos, splutniks, fools,
Culdees, bauldies, Trekkies, ghouls—
Airheids fae thi West Coast, steely knives and all,
welcome to thi Hotel Guillaume McGonagall.
We got: Imagists, bigamists, fowk dug up wi beakers,
lit.mag.eds, shit-thir-beds, and fans o thi New Seekers—
Doric loons wi Bothy tunes that ploo yir wits tae clay;
ut's open mike fur ony shite doon at thi Cabaret.

Alpha males ur no allowed
amang this outre-foutery crowd
tho gin they wear thir alphaboots
there's nane o us can keep thum oot,
and damn-aa wimmen care tae visit,
and nane o thum iver seem tae miss it:
gin you suspeck yir dick's too small
treh thi Cabaret McGonagall.

There's dum-dum boys wi wuiden heids
and Myrna Loy is snoggin Steed,
there's wan drunk wearin breeks he's peed—

naw—thon's thi Venerable Bede;
in fack thon auld scribe smells lyk ten o um,
he's no cheenged'iz habit i thi last millenium:
gin thi wits ye werr bourn wi hae stertit tae stall
treh thi Cabaret McGonagall.

We got: Loplops and robocops and Perry Comatose,
Cyclops and ZZ Top and fowk that pick thir nose—
Fare ye-weel and cheery-bye and bonne nuit tae you all,
thi booncirs think we ought tae leave thi Club McGonagall.
But we got: Moptops and bebop bats and Krapp's Last Tapeworm
    friends,
Swap-Shop vets and neurocrats, but damn-aa sapiens—
Arrevederchi Rothesay, atque vale tae thi Tay,
Eh wish that Eh hud ne'er set eye upon this Cabaret.

dottitt: daft, confused; oorie: dirty, tasteless; gowks: fools; ciamar
a thu: how are you (Gaelic). kelpies: river spirits in the shape
of horses; selkies: seals which can take on human form; leids:
languages. Culdees: members of the Columban church; loons:
young men; Both tunes: ballads from the rural North-East; plop:
plouh; foutery: excessively fussy.

Smirr

The leaves flick past the windows of the train
like feeding swifts: they're scooping up small mouth-
fuls of the midge-like autumn, fleeing south
with the train's hot wake: their feathers are small rain.
'Serein' they could say, where I'm passing through,
then just a sound could link rain with the leaves'
symptom, of being sere. But who deceives
themselves such rhyming leaps knit seasons now?
Some alchemist would get the point at once;

why I, against the leaves' example, try—
migrating to my cold roots like a dunce.
Thicker than needles sticking to a fir,
Winter is stitching mists of words with chance,
like smears of myrrh, like our small rain, our smirr.

The King and Queen of Dumfriesshire

The King and Queen of Dumfriesshire sit
in their battery-dead Triumph, gazing ahead
at an iced-over windscreen like a gull rolled flat.
They are cast in bronze, with Henry Moore holes
shot in each other by incessant argument;
these are convenient for holding her tartan flask,
his rolled-up Scotsman. The hairy skeleton
of a Border terrier sits in the back window,
not nodding. On the back seat rests
their favourite argument, the one about
how he does not permit her to see the old friends
she no longer likes and he secretly misses;
the one which is really about punishing each other
for no longer wanting to make love.
The argument is in the form of a big white bowl
with a black band around it hand-painted with fruit.
It has a gold rim, and in it lies
a brown curl of water from the leaking roof.
Outside, the clouds continue
to bomb the glen with sheep, which bare
their slate teeth as they tumble,
unexpectedly sneering.
The King and Queen of Dumfriesshire sit
like the too-solid bullet-ridden ghosts
of Bonny and Clyde, not eating their

tinned salmon sandwiches, crustless, still
wrapped in tinfoil, still in the tupperware.
They survey their domain, not glancing at
each other, not removing from the glove compartment
any of the old words they have always used.
Words like 'twae', like 'couthy', like 'Kirkcudbright',
which keep their only threat at bay: of separation.

⁊ SELIMA HILL

Selima Hill was born in London in 1945 and lives in Dorset. We often find Hill's characters abandoned in the most bizarre situations, but despite their initial wide-eyed bewilderment they usually turn out to be forceful agents. Hill has been one of the very few poets to have contributed something wholly original to the feminist debate in the last twenty years—though her imaginative project is far broader, and she has been a liberating influence on the poetry of both sexes. What sometimes looks like free association is often an effect in a carefully calculated and disturbed interior monologue; she often seems to dare the reader to conflate the 'I' of the poem with the poet's confession, which it clearly is not. This disturbing double-take often gives the work a thrillingly decentred and unstable quality.

FURTHER READING:
A Little Book of Meat (Bloodaxe, 1993), *Violet* (Bloodaxe, 1997)

I Will Be Arriving Next Thursday in My Wedding-Dress

I will be arriving next Thursday in my wedding-dress.
I will be arriving next Thursday morning
at seven o'clock
in a white satin wedding-dress
the colour and texture
of one-hundred-per-cent-fit Bull Terriers
that feel like eels;
he will hear me
calling his name across the waterfalls,
and, craning his neck
(he's as small as a small jockey),
he will suddenly see me
staring at him through his kitchen window—
my ankle-length satin wedding-dress
dragged over to one side by a large rucksack
containing nougat, maps
and a rocky island
crossed by the tracks of relays of stocky horses

carrying the world's fiercest
and most nimble seamstresses
towards a bed piled high for him and me
with eiderdowns that hold a million lips
peeled from the heads of skilfully-dried
small lovers.

I Know I Ought to Love You

I know I ought to love you
but it's hopeless.
Screaming is the best I can do.
I scream at you for such a long time
that even when I stop the scream goes on.
It screams between us like a frozen street
with stiff exhausted birds embedded in it.

My Sister's Jeans

My sixty-year-old 'forty-year-old' sister,
whose head I dream of floating muslin over,
acres of it, drenched in chloroform,
comes teetering down from the bathroom
in clouds of talc
where what she has done she has
squeezed herself into some shorts
so shockingly short they extrude her like polystyrene,
gleaming, insistent, discoloured, and up to no good,
and reeking of something,
and stuffed full of something alive,
of eyeballs, ferrets, cheeses, swelling hymns,
that she could no more come and sit down beside me in,

no more sit down anywhere in,
and become my sister again,
than a beautiful woman,
whose naked and suckable nipples probe the air
can shimmy up against a wall of mouths
and not be unstable.

A Small Hotel

My nipples tick
like little bombs of blood.

Someone is walking
in the yard outside.

I don't know why
Our Lord was crucified.

A really good fuck
makes me feel like custard.

Please Can I Have a Man

Please can I have a man who wears corduroy.
Please can I have a man
who knows the names of 100 different roses;
who doesn't mind my absent-minded rabbits
wandering in and out
as if they own the place,
who makes me creamy curries from fresh lemon-grass,
who walks like Belmondo in *A Bout de Souffle*;
who sticks all my carefully-selected postcards—

sent from exotic cities
he doesn't expect to come with me to,
but would if I asked, which I will do—
with nobody else's, up on his bedroom wall,
starting with Ivy, the Famous Diving Pig,
whose picture, in action, I bought ten copies of;
who talks like Belmondo too, with lips as smooth
and tightly-packed as chocolate-coated
(*melting* chocolate) peony buds;
who knows that piling himself stubbornly on top of me
like a duvet stuffed with library books and shopping-bags
is all too easy: please can I have a man
who is not prepared to do that.
Who is not prepared to say I'm 'pretty' either.
Who, when I come trotting in from the bathroom
like a squealing freshly-scrubbed piglet
that likes nothing better than a binge
of being affectionate and undisciplined and uncomplicated,
opens his arms like a trough for me to dive into.

∽ MICHAEL HOFMANN

Michael Hofmann was born in Freiberg, Germany, in 1957. He lives in London but also teaches at the University of Florida. Hofmann has the knack of divining, apparently effortlessly, the one scene or cinematic shot from a longer, unseen narrative where every tiny detail—though presented with an apparently arbitrary naturalism—seems to direct the reader to the same overwhelming conclusion. Hofmann's is an often terrifying straight and unblinking gaze; he has no interest in sparing feelings, least of all his own. In his commitment to the poetry of experience—and in his rigorous intellect and highly cultured imagination— Robert Lowell has found one of his truest disciples. Hofmann is also a fine and sometimes outspoken critic, and a distinguished translator from German.

FURTHER READING:
Acrimony (Faber & Faber, 1986), *Corona, Corona* (Faber & Faber, 1993)

Ancient Evenings

(for A.)

My friends hunted in packs, had themselves photographed
under hoardings that said 'Tender Vegetables'
or 'Big Chunks', but I had you—my Antonia!
Not for long, nor for a long time now . . .

Later, your jeans faded more completely,
and the hole in them wore to a furred square,
as it had to, but I remember my hands
skating over them, there where the cloth was thickest.

You were so quiet, it seemed like an invitation
to be disturbed, like Archimedes and the soldier,
like me, like the water displaced from my kettle
when I heated tins of viscous celery soup in it

until the glue dissolved and the labels crumbled
and the turbid, overheated water turned into more soup . . .

I was overheated, too. I could not trust my judgement.
The coffee I made in the dark was eight times too strong.

My humour was gravity, so I sat us both in an armchair
and toppled over backwards. I must have hoped
the experience of danger would cement our relationship.
Nothing was broken, and we made surprisingly little noise.

The Machine That Cried

'*Il n'y a pas de détail*'—Paul Valéry

When I learned that my parents were returning
to Germany, and that I was to be jettisoned,
I gave a sudden lurch into infancy and Englishness.
Carpets again loomed large in my world: I sought out
their fabric and warmth, where there was nowhere to fall . . .

I took up jigsaw puzzles, read mystical cricket thrillers
passing all understanding, even collected toy soldiers
and killed them with matchsticks fired from the World War One
field-guns I bought from Peter Oborn down the road
—he must have had something German, with that name—

who lived alone with his mother, like a man . . .
My classmates were equipped with sexual insults
for the foaming lace of the English women playing Wimbledon,
but I watched them blandly on our rented set
behind drawn curtains, without ever getting the point.

My building-projects were as ambitious as the Tower of Babel.
Something automotive of my construction limped across the floor
to no purpose, only lugging its heavy battery.

Was there perhaps some future for Christiaan Barnard,
or the electric car, a milk-float groaning like a sacred heart?

I imagined Moog as von Moog, a mad German scientist.
His synthesizer was supposed to be the last word in versatility,
but when I first heard it on Chicory Tip's
Son of my Father, it was just a unisono metallic drone,
five notes, as inhibited and pleonastic as the title.

My father bought a gramophone, a black box,
and played late Beethoven on it, which my mother was always
to associate with her miscarriage of that year.
I was forever carrying it up to my room,
and quietly playing through my infant collection of singles,

Led Zeppelin, The Tremoloes, *My Sweet Lord* . . .
The drums cut like a scalpel across the other instruments.
Sometimes the turntable rotated slowly, then everything
went flat, and I thought how with a little more care
it could have been all right. There again, so many things

were undependable . . . My first-ever British accent wavered
between Pakistani and Welsh. I called *Bruce's* record shop
just for someone to talk to. He said, 'Certainly, Madam'.
Weeks later, it was 'Yes, sir, you can bring your children'.
It seemed I had engineered my own birth in the new country.

The Late Richard Dadd, 1817–1886

The *Kentish Independent* of 1843
carried his pictures of his father, himself
and the scene of his crime. The first photo-journalist:
fairy-painter, father-slayer, poor, bad, mad Richard Dadd.

His extended Grand Tour took in the Holy Land
and ended in Bethlem Hospital, with its long panoptical
galleries, spider-plants, whippets and double-gaslights.
He had outlived himself at twenty-six . . .

There was one day he seemed to catch sunstroke.
He fancied the black, scorched beard of a sheik
would furnish him with some 'capital paintbrushes'.
Sailing up the Nile, on the *Hecate,*

they spent Christmas Day eating boiled eggs
and plum pudding, and playing cards for the captain's soul.
The temples at Luxor stood under a full moon, lightly boiled.
Sir Thomas got off to try and bag a crocodile.

The route up from Marseille went as the crow flies—
precipitately, a dash from ear to ear.
A fellow-traveller let him play with his collar and tie,
until he pulled out 'an excellent English razor'.

There was his watercolour, 'Dead Camel',
and a series of drawings of his friends,
all with their throats cut,
Frith, Egg, Dadd, Phillip and O'Neill.

He saw himself as a catspaw, Osiris's right-hand man
on earth. His digs in Newman Street
contained three hundred eggs, and the earth
cracked when he walked on it.

Lament for Crassus

Who grows old in fifty pages of Plutarch:
mores, omens, campaigns, Marius at sixty,
fighting fit, working out on the Campus Martius?

It surely isn't me, pushing thirty, taking a life a night,
my head on a bookshelf, five shelves of books overhead,
the bed either a classic or remaindered?

—I read about Crassus, who owned most of Rome.
Crassus, the third man, the third triumvir,
the second term in any calculation.

Crassus, the pioneer of insuranburn,
with his architect slaves and firefighter slaves,
big in silver, big in real estate, big in personnel.

Crassus, who had his name linked with a Vestal Virgin,
but was only after her house in the suburbs.
Crassus of bread and suburbs and circuses,

made Consul for his circuses, Crassus
impresario, not Crassus *imperator*, Crassus
who tried to break the military-political nexus.

Crassus, the inventor of the demi-pension holiday,
holed up in a cave on the coast of Spain for a month,
getting his dinner put out for him, and a couple of slave-girls.

Crassus, whose standards wouldn't rise on the final day,
who came out of his corner in careless black,
whose head was severed a day later than his son's.

ᴄᴠ KATHLEEN JAMIE

Kathleen Jamie was born in 1962 and grew up in Midlothian, Scotland. She now lives in Newburgh, Fife, and teaches at the University of St Andrews. Jamie has developed from a very young writer of great promise to one of the most significant figures now at work in the language. Her wholly unagonized meditations on our relationship with the world and one other argue for an almost Burnsian engagement with the whole being; recently her work has walked a fascinating line between a kind of eco-mysticism and a deep political engagement. Like Crawford and Herbert she occasionally writes in Scots; but while Scots seems to have almost provided another literary persona for those writers, Jamie's often seems purely a more intimate register of her English.

FURTHER READING:
The Queen of Sheba (Bloodaxe, 1994), *Jizzen* (Picador, 1999)

The Way We Live

Pass the tambourine, let me bash out praises
to the Lord God of movement, to Absolute
non-friction, flight, and the scarey side:
death by avalanche, birth by failed contraception.
Of chicken tandoori and reggae, loud, from tenements,
commitment, driving fast and unswerving
friendship. Of tee-shirts on pulleys, giros and Bombay,
barmen, dreaming waitresses with many fake-gold
bangles. Of airports, impulse, and waking to uncertainty,
to strip-lights, motorways, or that pantheon—
the mountains. To overdrafts and grafting

and the fit slow pulse of wipers as you're
creeping over Rannoch, while the God of moorland
walks abroad with his entourage of freezing fog,
his bodyguard of snow.
Of endless gloaming in the North, of Asiatic swelter,
to launderettes, anecdotes, passions and exhaustion,
Final Demands and dead men, the skeletal grip

of government. To misery and elation; mixed,
the sod and caprice of landlords.
To the way it fits, the way it is, the way it seems
to be: let me bash out praises—pass the tambourine.

The Bogey-Wife

She hoists her thigh over back fences,
her feet squash
worms, hands stained brown as dung.

She flusters hens, looking for babies:
one eye swivelling in the middle of her forehead,
leaves, like the yeti,
the proof of her footprint.

She's simple, gets tangled in the netting
of raspberry groves; but canny—keeps
to the railway wall, the kitchen-midden.

She can *smell* babies, will push
between laundry hung to dry
arms, strong as plum-boughs
twisting into fruit,

and the old wives run her out of town,
some banging pot-lids as others shout
This is private property! Ye've nae right!

But she is charming when cornered,
speaks a nice Scots,
wears a fresh T-shirt
and attractive batik trousers.

Skeins o Geese

Skeins o geese write a word
across the sky. A word
struck lik a gong
afore I wis born.
The sky moves like cattle, lowin.

I'm as empty as stane, as fields
ploo'd but not sown, naked
an blin as a stane. Blin
tae the word, blin
tae a' soon but geese ca'ing.

Wire twists lik archaic script
roon a gate. The barbs
sign tae the wind as though
it was deef. The word whustles
ower high for ma senses. Awa.

No lik the past which lies
strewn aroun. Nor sudden death.
No like a lover we'll ken
an connect wi forever.
The hem of its goin drags across the sky.

Whit dae birds write on the dusk?
A word niver spoken or read.
The skeins turn hame,
on the wind's dumb moan, a soun,
maybe human, bereft.

Pipistrelles

In the centre of the sheep-field
a stand of Douglas firs
hold between them, tenderly,
a tall enclosure, like a vase.

How could we have missed it
before today—just never seen
this clear, translucent vessel
tinted like citrine?

What we noticed were pipstrelles:
cinder-like, friable; flickering
the place hained by trees
till the air seemed to quicken,

and the bats were a single
edgy intelligence, testing an idea
for a new form,
which unfolded, cohered

before our eyes. The world's
mind is such interstices; cells
charging with cool dawn light;
—is that what they were telling us?

—but they vanished, suddenly,
before we'd understood,
and the trees grew in a circle,
elegant and mute.

The Hill-track

But for her green
palpitating throat, they lay
inert as stone, the male
clamped like a package
to her back. They became

as you looked, almost
beautiful, she mottled
to leafy brown, his back
marked with two stripes,
pale as over-wintered grass.

When he bucked, once,
neither even blinked;
their oval, gold-lined eyes
held to some bog-dull
imperative. The car

that would smear them
into one, belly
to belly, tongue thrust
utterly into soft brain,
approached and pressed on

oh how we press on—
the car and passengers, the slow
creatures of this earth,
the woman by the verge
with her hands cupped.

✑ ALAN JENKINS

Alan Jenkins was born in London in 1955 and now works as an editor. Jenkins's earlier work showed the strong influence of Paul Muldoon and Peter Reading, but he has emerged as a distinctive and very English voice. Jenkins is a particularly fine elegist, and like Michael Hofmann a sometimes uncomfortably unflinching observer of human behaviour, especially his own. These are, in the end—despite the air of braggadocio or insouciance Jenkins sometimes feigns to wrongfoot the reader—disarming poems of considerable grace, honesty, and humility, and Jenkins's confidence and range grows with each new book.

FURTHER READING:
Harm (Chatto & Windus, 1994), *The Drift* (Chatto & Windus, 2000)

Visiting

He visited, the man who takes your life
and turns it upside-down, from floor
to ceiling; and he saw I had no wife,
and saw the things that I had worked hard for
and smiled, as if he knew what went on *here*.

He visited the corner of my flat
where daily I had spooned out food
for my dainty-footed, air-sniffing cat
and through the summer, chunks left half-chewed
had poured rich smells into the atmosphere.

Flies visited the smells. They hung in heat
like helicopters seen from a distance,
they drooled and fed on rotting processed meat,
they laid their eggs. The buzzing small insistence
should have warned me, the cat not going near.

Friends visited, but no-one noticed anything.
And when he tore my carpet up, the man—

No lie, I nearly puked my ring.
I saw yellow-white seethe in a silver can
full of dank sawdust, a towpath by a weir—

I visited my father on the bank
where he and I went fishing each week-end;
the shrubs, the weir, the lock and river shrank,
our bicycles had vanished round a bend
and a high tide taken all our gear.

I visited my father in the pubs
where I had watched him drink away the hours
of talk or silence, piling up the stubs
in ashtrays, but the cigarettes were sour
and the bitter had an aftertaste of fear.

Portrait of a Lady

She's been in too deep and out too far, oh *man*,
her dark eyes spill nearly twenty years of bruises,
roll-ups and cider, and a battered Morris van
holds everything she ever wants or uses—
her Dylan tapes, her Steeleye Span and Fleetwood Mac
(he told her once she looked like Stevie Nicks,
and 'Go Your Own Way' still takes her back),
her daughter's scribbles, her I-Ching spill-sticks,
the bag of grass hand-picked from her veggie patch,
some tattered old Viragos, Mervyn Peakes
and a book of newish poetry. There's a catch
in her voice as she half-sings, half-speaks
of the slow blues she wrote about him when he left,
that neither of you will remember by the morning
when you have to leave as well and she offers you a lift
through dripping lanes—but it draws you, yawning,

shivering, to huddle in the pile of blankets, quilts
while she clings close, and seems on the edge
of tears; your breath, the frost-blurred ghosts and guilts . . .
We're gonna meet, she tells you, *meet on the ledge.*

Barcelona

What was I doing here, haunting the dead?
From his studio in a derelict cigarette factory
the windowless windows of the derelict warehouse opposite
were blind eyes overlooking the ochres and umbers
of his palette—I saw his corduroys and scarf,
his slicked-back hair, his head thrown back to laugh
a nineteenth-century, *La Bohème* laugh. But he was gone
and I sniffed stale air for a word I could use,
a word for his life, his art, for the night he went
to be chosen to die by a thing he did not choose,
did not see . . . It was late, I wanted to go to bed
with his beautiful German widow, but she talked me
into submission and downstairs to the *calle*
where someone was shouting and waving a knife
at a woman, his girlfriend, model, wife . . .
Back on the Rambla there was safety in numbers,
or so I thought. I wanted you. It was your scent
I'd caught, wandering by day around the gothic quarter
where you had struggled through a 'difficult' year
on a language-teacher's wage; I'd joined the throng
in the cathedral cloister, stood below its vault
of tattered palms and counted seven fat white geese
that gobble-squabbled under them, for crumbs, for release,
then at my hotel in the little square
I'd sat with chestnut blossom falling in my beer
and imagined it falling in your hair;

when I had to eat, I'd breathed in every tapas bar
the now-familiar amalgam that you are—
the sweet, the garlicky-pungent and the salt—
and remembered you come dripping from the water
for me to frame in the crook of your freckled arm
our cubist village and its single palm,
our spaghetti-western beach, deserted for a shoot-out
at high noon, when the sunlight struck it like a gong.
I'd remembered how I 'wore my impatience on my sleeve'.
But what was this drift or shift, like condom-littered sands
along the shore? This searching fingers of left hands
for seals of ownership, and hiding old defeats?
I was heading for the waterfront—God's truth—
to drink in its wind-braced, salt-stiffened air
when the Rambla caught me in its wave and bore me on
to a little, red-lit, low-lit booth
where I watched two strangers—brisk,
methodical, expressionless—ride out their storm;
slap, slap, he ploughed her salty furrow, warm
and wet and open wide, he gave no thought to risk
as he poured ambergris into her waiting mouth—
and tugging at myself, so raw and dry,
I wanted to believe, in art that doesn't die,
in whatever lives on in a gothic-baroque-cubist heaven
with sea-nymphs riding dolphins, sea-creatures, shells,
with clouds and putti, far from these semen smells,
blade-and-needle-sharpened, blind-eyed streets.

Inheritance

Herring-bone and fern, this coat
materialized on the grouse-moor,
on ground my self-made great-grandfather treads

ten years before the First World War;
shotgun-cartridges, tobacco-shreds
and dry-flies in the pocket of his coat,

and the slender hip-flask,
silver in its leather sleeve,
tarnished now from trying to relieve
my grandfather's thirst, take off his fear
of rats and snipers and the feeble cheer
that goes up as they go over. Last-nip flask.

On the way to art-school dances
or a Left Book Club lecture (Spain)
my father glances at his gold-plated watch
and slips the flask, half-full of scotch,
back in the pocket of his coat. At Alamein
it stops a shrapnel-shard as he advances

and he comes home, when the war is ended,
to a place where quiet lives are led
(grandfather, father both long dead,
grouse-moor and money all long gone);
a wife and kids are all he gambles on
but some things, like the fence, are never mended.

And he gives me, not yet twenty,
the flask, that I will later lose,
the coat and watch, that I will wear and use
to seem a man in the world I have not fought for,
worked for, even spared much though for.
This is my inheritance. It is plenty.

ᴄᴏ JACKIE KAY

Jackie Kay was born in Edinburgh, Scotland in 1962 and now lives in Manchester, England. Kay tackles some uncomfortable subjects with deceptive good humour and light music that often serve only to soften the reader for the punch. Kay is a keen observer of the more intimate human conflicts and is attracted again and again to the frontlines of community, family, and love. Her poems that address issues of prejuduce and inequality are often all the more powerful for their com-passionate portrayal of both victim and perpetrator; this power of imaginative empathy is also strongly evident in her fine work as a novelist.

FURTHER READING:
Other Lovers (Bloodaxe, 1993), *Off Colour* (Bloodaxe, 1998)

Even the Trees

Even the trees outside feel it, their fine branches
their sixth sense of mercy,

they bend into the wind and ask for forgiveness
to come in a storm,

and join the congregation of silence; that tall witness.
One man, tied to a tree and whipped

never worked again in the cotton fields. In the early
light, the delicate bone-light

that broke hearts, a song swept from field to field;
a woman's memory paced centuries,

down and down, a blue song in the beat of her heart,
in an old car that crossed

a railroad track; the scream of a warning—
is that why we remember certain things and not others;

the sound of the bass, the sound of the whip, the strange
strangled wind, bruises floating through light air

like leaves and landing, landing, here; this place.
Everything that's happened once could happen again.

In my country

walking by the waters
down where an honest river
shakes hands with the sea,
a woman passed round me
in a slow watchful circle,
as if I were a superstition;

or the worst dregs of her imagination,
so when she finally spoke
her words spliced into bars
of an old wheel. A segment of air.
Where do you come from?
'Here', I said, 'Here. These parts'.

Finger

What is it made of? Guilt. Blame. Sometimes,
as if pain demands I point a finger—
one of the terminal members of my hand.

This instrument; this fine tune. Listen.
I know which notes will strike a chord.
I use my fingers as a measure.

Like the pointed sheaths of a reaping machine;
the bit the knife comes through to cut corn.
Simply: flesh, blood, marrow, bone?

There is no room for conversation; no other questions
to ask. Nothing to do, but say: That was wrong.
How big was the slave's room?

Have you been to the plantation? Tobacco. Sugar.
The quarters—the temperature of a hot house. Plants.
The placing of plants in a soil so they may grow.

Breeding in the dead heat of a tiny room for the master.
Or him groping you as your man stands by.
And him fingering the money.

And me, a songster, marking music, the strange colour
I will play soon in the wooden holes. Plantation.
The skin growing on trees. Listen.

Watch the way my fingers move across your temple.
Answer me. They say it doesn't exist anymore.
This is another century. Take my fingerprint.

The Shoes of Dead Comrades

On my father's feet are the shoes of dead comrades.
Gifts from the comrades' sad red widows.
My father would never see good shoes go to waste.

Good brown leather, black leather, leather soles.
Doesn't matter if they are a size too big, small.

On my father's feet are the shoes of dead comrades.
The marches they marched against Polaris. UCS.
Everything they ever believed tied up with laces.
A cobbler has replaced the sole, the heel.
Brand new, my father says, look, feel.

On my father's feet are the shoes of dead comrades.
These are in good nick. These were pricey.
Italian leather. See that. Lovely.
He always was a classy dresser was Arthur.
Ever see Wullie dance? Wullie was a wonderful waltzer.

On my father's feet are the shoes of dead comrades.
It scares me half to death to consider
that one day it won't be Wullie or Jimmy or Arthur,
that one day someone will wear the shoes of my father,
the brown and black leather of all the dead comrades.

[from] Other Lovers

What was it you said again there by the river

And later, when the young danced to an old song,
the moon split in two, the stars smashed,
what was it again?

By the river, by the procession of trees,
the shadow marching across your face,
how deep do you feel?

I hold the light between us. Kiss you
hard in the dark. Ahead of us, the bright blue eyes of sheep.
Are there words for this? Words that sink to the bottom

of the river where ducks flap their sudden wings,
startle silence; believe me, believe me.
We walk this night, shining our bright eye ahead.
Do you love me, love me, do you.

✣ GWYNETH LEWIS

Gwyneth Lewis was born in Cardiff, Wales, in 1959 and has worked in television production. Lewis is our foremost Welsh poet and writes in both Welsh and English. Her poems, however, find their incarnation in one or the other language, and interestingly Lewis tends not to translate between them. The Welsh language and its precarious condition are recurrent themes; but Lewis's considerable technical deftness allows her to tackle a remarkably broad range of subjects. She is also capable of a highly confident comedy, and in common with many Celtic writers, unafraid to mix the comic and the grave within the same poem, when others seem to regard these registers as almost different genres.

FURTHER READING:
Zero Gravity (Bloodaxe, 1998), *Parables & Faxes* (Bloodaxe, 1995)

Pentecost

The Lord wants me to go to Florida.
I shall cross the border with the mercury thieves,
as foretold in the faxes and prophecies,
and the checkpoint angel of Estonia
will have alerted the uniformed birds
to act unnatural and distract the guards

so I pass unhindered. My glossolalia
shall be my passport—I shall taste the tang
of travel on the atlas of my tongue—
salt Poland, sour Denmark and sweet Vienna
and all men in the Spirit shall understand
that, in His wisdom, the Lord has sent

a slip of a girl to save great Florida.
I shall tear through Europe like a standing flame,
not pausing for long, except to rename
the occasional city; in Sofia
thousands converted and hundred slain
in the Holy Spirit along the Seine.

My life is your chronicle; O Florida
revived, look forward to your past,
and prepare your perpetual Pentecost
of golf course and freeway, shopping mall and car
so the fires that are burning in the orange groves
turn light into sweetness and the huddled graves

are hives of the future—an America
spelt plainly, translated in the Everglades
where palm fruit hang like hand grenades
ready to rip whole treatises of air.
Then the S in the tail of the crocodile
will make perfect sense to the bibliophile

who will study this land, his second Torah.
All this was revealed. Now I wait for the Lord
to move heaven and earth to send me abroad
and fulfil His bold promise to Florida.
As I stay put, He shifts His continent:
Atlantic closes, the sheet of time is rent.

'One day, feeling hungry'

One day, feeling hungry, I swallowed the moon.
It stuck, like a wafer, to the top of my mouth,
dry as an aspirin. It slowly went down,

showing the gills of my vocal cords,
the folded wings in my abdomen,
the horrible twitch of my insect blood.

Lit from inside, I stood alone
(dark to myself) but could see from afar
the brightness of others who had swallowed stars.

Woods

Midwinter and this beech wood's mind
is somewhere else. Like fallen light

snow's broken glass fills up the furrows.
Nothing that doesn't have to moves.

We walk through a frozen waterfall
of boles, all held in vertical

except for the careful woodpile laid
in pencils across a tidied glade.

Look back and from the place we were
a bird calls out because we're not there,

a double note whose range expands,
pushing the line where our racket ends

out ever further. That elaborate song
can only exist because we're gone.

A vandal, I shatter that place with a stone.
The bird is for silence. I am for home.

The Flaggy Shore

(for Nora Nolan)

Even before I've left, I long
for this place. For hay brought in before the rain,
its stooks like stanzas, for glossy cormorants
that make metal eyes and dive like hooks,

fastening the bodice of the folding tide
which unravels in gardens of carraigín.
I walk with the ladies who throw stones at the surge
and their problems, don't answer the phone
in the ringing kiosk. Look. In the clouds
hang pewter promontories, long bays
whose wind-indented silent coasts
make me homesick for where I've not been.
Quicksilver headlands shoot into the night
till distance and the dying of day
dull steel and vermilion to simple lead
blown downward to the dark, then out of sight.

ix Advice on Adultery
[from] Welsh Espionage

The first rule is to pacify the wives
if you're presented as the golden hope
at the office party. You're pure of heart,
but know the value of your youthful looks.
Someone comments on your lovely back.
Talk to the women, and avoid the men.

In work they treat you like one of the men
and soon you're bored with the talk of the wives
who confide in you about this husband's back,
or that husband's ulcer. They sincerely hope
you'll never have children . . . it ruins your looks.
And did you know David has a dicky heart?

You go to parties with a beating heart,
start an affair with one of the men.
The fact you've been taking good care of your looks
doesn't escape the observant wives

who stare at you sourly. Cross your fingers and hope
that no one's been talking behind your back.

A trip to the Ladies. On your way back
one of them stops you for a heart to heart.
She hesitates, then expresses the hope
that you won't take offence, but men will be men,
and a young girl like you, with such striking looks. . . .
She's heard nasty rumours from some of the wives.

She knows you're innocent, but the wives,
well, jump to conclusions from the way it looks. . . .
In a rage, you resolve she won't get him back,
despite the pressure from the other wives.
They don't understand . . . you'll stick with the men,
only they are *au fait* with affairs of the heart.

You put it to him that you're living in hope.
He grants that you're beautiful, but looks
aren't everything. He's told the men,
who smirk and wink. So now you're back
to square one, but with a broken heart.
You make your peace with the patient wives.

Don't give up hope at the knowing looks.
Get your own back, have a change of heart:
Ignore the men, start sleeping with the wives.

᧞ RODDY LUMSDEN

Roddy Lumsden was born in 1966 in St Andrews, Scotland, and now lives in Bristol. Lumsden's poems are performances; he is interested in how far one can take the idea of the poem as 'entertainment', and the artifice of the poem is nearly always kept before the reader's eyes. This device is often cleverly used to disguise a confessional streak in his work and pass it off as a kind of ludic excess. That moments of considerable lyricism so often emerge is a great tribute to Lumsden's control of voice and register; he is capable of impressively fast and smooth gear changes, and can switch between the comic and lyric in the space of a line, to disarming effect.

FURTHER READING:
Yeah Yeah Yeah (Bloodaxe,1997), *The Book of Love* (Bloodaxe,2000)

Always

After the full-day's westward drive you find
the house familiar from a photograph,
its brass-hung door thrown wide.

A meeting party welcomes you: up front,
the matriarch, corn hair tied in a bunch,
the husband of few words

and, in behind two sniffly, smutty boys
you'll take a good few days to tell apart,
a gran'ma, blunt and blouse.

It's then that you sense her, in and down the hall,
so vague, at first you take her for a shadow
or portrait on the wall,

the daughter who, that night, will steal in slow
to visit you with kisses coarse and sweet,
to gift you with her heat,

and who through the remainder of the week
won't speak again, although you send her notes,
whose name you never know.

And always this will whittle at your wits—
the way she gave her nightdress to the floor,
one finger to her lips

to call aboard the silence of the land
to forge the night-time colours in her hair—
until you grow unsure

of what was real and what was in the wind,
of all that being meant before and since
that single word she said.

An Older Woman

Mid-1990s, Scotland, dead of winter
And more than old enough to be my mother.
She hailed a taxi in the city centre,
Dropped me off a hundred yards before her
And we were naked fifteen minutes later;
A Brookes & Simmons dress, her bra and knickers
Were delicate and in contrasting colours.
I didn't stop to think if there were others,
Responded prompt and proudly to her orders.
And now I wish to speak to celebrate her
Although I don't know anything about her
Except the spray of freckles on her shoulders
And that she said the world revolved around her.
I know exactly what to do without her.

Piquant

Just as, surely, sweat is consommé
or scallions scowled in a jelly-pan
or golden acid, wrathful in a stoppered jar

and other body fluids I shan't mention
are sulphur, globster, stinkhorn, horse or Brie,
then there are these late-on summer days

when, just where nostril meets the upper lip,
a film appears, part sweat, part oil
with a perfect, clean white chocolate smell,

two parts ginger to ninety-eight parts milk
and which, when I lean in to take this kiss,
says *fool for sugar,* says *mammals one and all,*

says *never again a love like this.*

The Man I Could Have Been

The man I could have been works for a vital institution, *is* a vital
    institution.
Without him, walls will crumble, somewhere, paint will peel.
He takes a catch.
He is outdoorsy and says *It was a nightmare* and means the traffic.
He's happy to watch a film and stops short of living in one.

The man I could have been owns a Subaru pickup the colour of
    cherry tomatoes.
He's in the black, not in the dark.
His mother is calm.

Women keep his baby picture in the windownooks of wallets.
No one dies on him.

The man I could have been owns bits of clothes not worn by
    uncles first.
He has no need of medicine.
He walks from Powderhall to Newington in twenty minutes.
He plays the piano *a little.*
Without him, havens buckle, sickbeds bloom.

The man I could have been lives locally.
He is quietly algebraic.
Without him, granite will not glister.
And when he sees a crisis, he does not dive in feet first.
He votes, for he believes in their democracy.

The man I could have been has a sense of direction.
For him, it was never Miss Scarlet with the dagger in the kitchen.
He knows his tilth and sows his seed.
He'll make a father.
He is no maven nor a connoisseur.

The man I could have been has a season ticket at Tynecastle.
He comes in at night and puts on *The Best of U2.*
He browses.
He puts fancy stuff in his bathwater.
He doesn't lace up his life with secrets.

The man I could have been was born on a high horse.
He knows the story of the Willow Pattern.
He had a dream last night you'd want to hear about
and remembers the words to songs.
His back is a saddle where lovers have ridden.

The man I could have been has a sovereign speech in him he's yet
    to give.
He might well wrassle him a bear.
He is a man about town.
He has the exact fare on him.
Without him, motley trauma.

The man I could have been, he learns from my mistakes.
He never thought it would be you.
And no one says *he's looking rather biblical.*
He has no need of London
and walks the middle of the road for it is his.

The man I could have been is quick and clean.
He is no smalltown Jesus nor a sawdust Caesar.
Without him, salt water would enter your lungs.
He doesn't hear these endless xylophones.
That's not him lying over there.

Glyn Maxwell was born in Welwyn Garden City in 1962 and now lives in New York. Maxwell made a huge impact when he first appeared on the UK scene, his style a remarkable chimera which seemed to have derived its narrative lyric from Bob Dylan, its delivery from Robert Frost, and its syntax from early Auden. Maxwell is a more difficult and experimental poet than many had imagined, and his obsessions are sometimes his alone; but his recent work shows a deepening concern with the contemporary mores, and in that project Frost seems to be emerging as his true exemplar. Despite this, his voice has developed into one of the most original of the last fifty years, and more and more seems to seek a kind of democratic clarity that has lost nothing of its early rhetorical force.

FURTHER READING:
Rest for the Wicked (Bloodaxe, 1995), *The Nerve* (Picador, 2002)

My Turn

I have been so enchanted by the girls
who have a hunch. I have been seen

following them to the red and green
see-saws. There have been a few of them

I recognised. I have been recognised.
I have stood on the roundabout and turned.

I have swung, uselessly, not as high as them.
Then seen the parents coming, and the rain

on rusty and unmanned remaining things.
I have calculated west from the light cloud.

Cried myself dry and jumped
back on the roundabout when it had stopped.

Started it again, in the dark wet,
with my foot down, then both my feet on it.

The Poem Recalls the Poet

This is for him, the writer, him I term
the creature of two feet, for he'd present
his face two feet away. He made a warm
glow to see by, willing and well meant,
but not, I'd have to say, for the long haul.
Things he began were things I'd have to end,
I sensed immediately. When I recall
the touch of what he did with his near hand,

the mood comes over me, but the mood goes,
and that reminds me too. November days
the thought of him resolves into a voice
that states it matters now—so does the wind,
but neither moves a muscle of my face
before it dies as if it read my mind.

Helene and Heloise

So swim in the embassy pool in a tinkling breeze
The sisters, *mes cousines*, they are blonde-haired
    Helene and Heloise,
One for the fifth time up to the diving board,
The other, in her quiet shut-eye sidestroke
Slowly away from me though I sip and look.

From in the palace of shades, inscrutable, cool,
I watch exactly what I want to watch

From by this swimming pool,
Helene's shimmer and moss of a costume, each
Soaking pony-tailing of the dark
And light mane of the littler one as they walk;

And the splash that bottles my whole life to today,
The spray fanning to dry on the porous sides,
    What these breathtakers say
In their, which is my, language but their words:
These are the shots the sun could fire and fires,
Is paid and drapes across the stretching years.

Now Heloise will dive, the delicate slimmer,
Calling Helene to turn who turns to see
    One disappearing swimmer
Only and nods, leans languorously away
To prop on the sides before me and cup her wet
Face before me near where I'd pictured it.

I was about to say I barely know them.—
I turn away because and hear of course
    Her push away. I see them
In my rose grotto of thought, and it's not a guess,
How they are, out of the water, out
In the International School they lie about,

What they can buy in the town, or the only quarters
Blondes can be seen alighting in, and only
    As guided shaded daughters
Into an acre of golden shop. 'Lonely'?
Who told me this had told me: 'They have no lives.
They will be children. Then they will be wives'.

Helene shrieks and is sorry—I don't think—my
Ankles cool with the splash of her sister's dive:
    I wave and smile and sigh.

Thus the happiest falling man alive,
And twenty-five, and the wetness and the brown
Hairs of my shin can agree, and I settle down.

'Already the eldest—suddenly—the problems.
The other draws, writes things'. I had heard
    Staccato horrid tantrums
Between earshot and the doorbell, held and read
Heloise's letters in chancery
Script to her dead grandmother, to me,

To nobody. They have a mother and father,
And love the largest pandas in the whole
    World of Toys. The other
Sister rang from Italy and all was well,
But wouldn't come this time. 'She'll never come.
She has a home. They do not have a home'.

Stretching out in her shiny gold from the pool,
Heloise swivels, and sits and kicks
    Then reaches back to towel
Her skinny shoulders tanned in a U of lux-
Uriant material. Helene
Goes slowly to the board, and hops again

Into the dazzle and splosh and the quiet. Say,
Two, three miles from here there are heaps of what,
    Living things, decay,
The blind and inoculated dead, and a squad
Of infuriated coldly eyeing sons
Kicking the screaming oath out of anyone's.

Cauchemar.—We will be clear if of course apart,
To London again me, they to their next
    Exotic important spot,
Their chink and pace of Gloucestershire, Surrey, fixed

Into the jungles, ports or the petrol deserts.
I try but don't see another of these visits;

As I see Helene drying, Heloise dry,
The dark unavoidable servant seeming to have
    Some urgency today
And my book blank in my hands. What I can love
I love encircled, trapped and I love free.
That happens to, and happens to be, me,

But this is something else. Outside the fence,
It could—it's the opposite—be a paradise
    Peopled with innocents,
Each endowed with a light inimitable voice,
Fruit abundant, guns like dragons and giants
Disbelieved, sheer tolerance a science—

Still, I'd think of Helene, of Heloise
Moving harmless, shieldless into a dull
    And dangerous hot breeze,
With nothing but hopes to please, delight, fulfil
Some male as desperate and as foul as this is,
Who'd not hurt them for all their limited kisses.

ᴄᴠ JAMIE McKENDRICK

Jamie McKendrick was born in Liverpool in 1955 and now lives in Oxford. Despite the Scottish name, McKendrick is an unmistakably English poet—self-perplexed, somehow melancholic in tone even when being humorous, he writes with a beautifully understated poise and a lightly worn but highly acute and scholarly intelligence. His poems are also full of stories and anecdote and distinguished by the beautiful and effortlessly symmetrical arcs of their arguments. He is one of our most cultured voices, in the best possible sense; as steeped in the European tradition as older poets such as Anthony Hecht and Peter Porter.

FURTHER READING:
Sky Nails: Selected Poems (Faber & Faber, 2000)

Ancient History

The year began with baleful auguries:
comets, eclipses, tremors, forest fires,
the waves lethargic under a coat of pitch
the length of the coastline. And a cow spoke,
which happened last year too, although last year
no one believed cows spoke. Worse was to come.
There was a bloody rain of lumps of meat
which flocks of gulls snatched in mid-air
while what they missed fell to the ground
where it lay for days without festering.
Then a wind tore up a forest of holm-oaks
and jackdaws pecked the eyes from sheep.
Officials construing the Sibylline books
told of helmeted aliens occupying
the crossroads, and high places of the city.
Blood might be shed. Avoid, they warned,
factions and in-fights. The tribunes claimed
this was the usual con-trick
trumped up to stonewall the new law
about to be passed. Violence was only curbed

by belief in a rumour that the tribes
to the east had joined forces and forged
weapons deadlier than the world has seen
and that even then the hooves of their scouts
had been heard in the southern hills.
The year ended fraught with the fear of war.
Next year began with baleful auguries.

Sky Nails

That first day, to break me in,
my hardened comrades
sent me scampering like a marmoset
from the topmost parapet

to the foreman's hut
for a bag of sky nails.
The foreman wondered which precise
shade of blue I had in mind.

It's still sky nails I need today
with their faint threads
and unbreakable heads

that will nail anything
to nothing
and make it stay.

Six Characters in Search of Something

A friend of mine met the son of a man
who it seems was eaten by a polar bear

in Iceland where the bear had stepped ashore
rafted from Greenland on an ice-floe.

The father of the man who met my friend
saw the bear who'd eat him loitering near
the shore and hurried on and met another man
who was walking the other way towards the bear.

He gave that other man his walking stick
but the bear meanwhile had doubled back
and reappeared on the path ahead
of the man who now was unprotected.

There may be a moral in this story
for the man, his son, the man he met,
for my friend, for me, or even for the bear,
but if there is it's better left unsaid.

The One-Star

for Michael Hofmann

Moving away in the taxi, I could just see myself
    climbing the marble steps and stepping through
    the plate-glass into a lounge-cum-vestibule,

its floor inlaid with a pink star of mineral grains
    and roughage—a breakfast for the afterlife.
    Beaded oak cladding, electrified oil-lamps,

a pharaonic desk-clerk. The air was cut and dried
    as though reconstituted in the basement's lungs
    and laid out, and folded, in cool dry reams.

The Shining was obtainable on the video service
   but would be scrambled after several minutes
   if you failed to press the 'Confirm' button

—otherwise it was a sex film I was embarrassed
   for the glamorous Thai receptionist
   to know I was watching. So I tried to read

The Temptation to Exist feeling conspicuously
   absent and uneasily aware
   of being ironed flat, flatter, by the clean sheets

and of the bedside table's inbuilt clock
   with its defective digits: every minute
   was a minus sign or a gnomon, every hour

was missing a slant side to its parallelogram.
   I closed the eyelids of the two nightlights;
   then mine . . . until I woke as though I'd feasted

on finely-ground enamel. There was nothing for it
   but to go home—some home!—but first why not
   spirit away the bar of opalescent soap, the small

urn of bath-foam and the shroud-sewing kit
   the size of a matchbook, with loops of thread
   five different shades of grey

or maybe it was the light? I had a good mind
   to mend the inside lining of my coat
   but instead went down in the shiny lift

and sank in an armchair by the crystal ashtray.
   Was I a Mr John Ashbery, someone asked me.
   No, I replied, not Mr Ashbery

—but pausing mysteriously mid-sentence as I felt
  he deserved a couple more guesses for being
  somehow on the right track, if not exactly warm.

The pause obviously disturbed him. He didn't
  like that pause. Well tell him
  if you'd be so kind that his taxi's waiting.

Oh yes I could just see myself doing that.

✏ ANDREW MOTION

Andrew Motion was born in London in 1952. Motion was a controversial choice for Poet Laureate after the death of Ted Hughes, but has confounded the doubters by emerging as the most energetic and forceful advocate for the art the post has seen. His official laureate poems (perhaps a near-impossible commission for any contemporary poet) have been marked with a good humour and grace, but he has also proven himself unafraid to refuse to toe the party line and has written poems openly critical of government policy. Despite his reputation as a narrativist, his best work is in lyric and elegy and is always marked by its open and confessional honesty, and a very sharp eye for the peripheral but ultimately telling detail.

FURTHER READING:
Selected Poems 1976–1997 (Faber & Faber, 1998)

The Lines

November, and the Sunday twilight fallen
dark at four—its hard unbroken rain
battering the garden. Vacantly I fill
this first week-end alone with anything—

the radio, a paperback you never read:
In 1845 200,000 navvies, 3,000 miles of line.
Lost faces lift—*a mania, a human alligator,*
shovels clinking under a high midsummer sun.

The heat-haze dances meadowsweet and may,
whole cliffs collapse, and line by line
I bring your death to lonely hidden villages,
red-tiled farms, *helpless women and timid men.*

A Wall

I have forgotten whatever
it was I wanted to say,
also the way I wanted
to say it. Form and music.

I should just look at the things
that are, and fix myself
to the earth. This wall,
facing me over the street,

smooth as a shaven chin
but pocked with holes
that scaffolders left,
and flicked with an over-

flow flag. Which still
leaves pigeon-shit,
rain-streaks, washing.
Or maybe it's really

a board where tiny
singing meteors strike?
I rest my case. I rest
my case and cannot imagine

hunger greater than this.
For marks.
For messages sent by hand.
For signs of life

A Glass of Wine

Exactly as the setting sun
clips the heel of the garden,

exactly as a pigeon
roosting tries to sing
and ends up moaning,

exactly as the ping
of someone's automatic carlock
dies into a flock
of tiny echo aftershocks,

a shapely hand of cloud
emerges from the crowd
of airy nothings that the wind allowed
to tumble over us all day
and points the way

towards its own decay,
but not before
a final sunlight-shudder pours
away across our garden floor

so steadily, so slow,
it shows you everything you need to know
about this glass I'm holding out to you,

its white, unblinking eye
enough to bear the whole weight of the sky.

The Letter

If I remember right, his first letter.
Found where? My side-plate perhaps,
or propped on our heavy brown tea-pot.
One thing is clear—my brother leaning
across asking *Who is he?* half angry
as always that summer before enlistment.

Then alone in the sunlit yard, mother
unlocking a door to call *Up so early?*
—waving her yellow duster goodbye
in a small sinking cloud. The gate creaks
shut and there in the lane I am running
uphill, vanishing where the woodland starts.

The Ashground. A solid contour swept
through ripening wheat, and fringe
of stippled green shading the furrow.
Now I am hardly breathing, gripping
the thin paper and reading *Write to me.*
Write to me please. I miss you. My angel.

Almost shocked, but repeating him line
by line, and watching the words jitter
under the pale spidery shadows of leaves.
How else did I leave the plane unheard
so long? But suddenly there it was—
a Messerschmitt low at the wood's edge.

What I see today is the window open,
the pilot's unguarded face somehow
closer than possible. Goggles pushed up,
a stripe of ginger moustache, and his eyes

fixed on my own while I stand
with the letter held out, my frock blowing,

before I am lost in cover again,
heading for home. He must have banked
at once, climbing steeply until his jump
and watching our simple village below—
the Downs swelling and flattening, speckled
with farms and bushy chalk-pits. By lunch

they found where he lay, the parachute
tight in its pack, and both hands spread
as if they could break the fall. I still
imagine him there exactly. His face pressed
close to the sweet-smelling grass. His legs
splayed wide in a candid unshamable V.

Mythology

Earth's axle creaks; the year jolts on; the trees
begin to slip their brittle leaves, their flakes of rust;
and darkness takes the edge off daylight, not
because it wants to—never that. Because it must.

And you? Your life was not your own to keep
or lose. Beside the river, swerving underground,
the future tracked you, snapping at your heels:
Diana, breathless, hunted by your own quick hounds.

ᨳ SEAN O'BRIEN

Sean O'Brien was born in London in 1952 and grew up in Hull. O'Brien is the UK's leading poet-critic, and a coveted name-check on every poet's dust-jacket. He is also one of the most fluent and articulate natural talents to have emerged since W. H. Auden. O'Brien's favourite voice is one of the most instantly identifiable in UK poetry today—Latinate, often written in relentless anapaests, with an obsessive draw towards the urban and suburban dystopias, where he finds a very black romance. Recent work has also reflected his growing interest in song-form and verse drama.

FURTHER READING:
Cousin Coat: Selected Poems 1976-2001 (Picador, 2002)

Cousin Coat

You are my secret coat. You're never dry.
You wear the weight and stink of black canals.
Malodorous companion, we know why
It's taken me so long to see we're pals,
To learn why my acquaintance never sniff
Or send me notes to say I stink of stiff.

But you don't talk, historical bespoke.
You must be worn, be intimate as skin,
And though I never lived what you invoke,
At birth I was already buttoned in.
Your clammy itch became my atmosphere,
An air made half of anger, half of fear.

And what you are is what I tried to shed
In libraries with Donne and Henry James.
You're here to hear a message from the dead
Whose history's dishonoured with their names.
You mean the North, the poor, and troopers sent
To shoot down those who showed their discontent.

No comfort there for comfy meliorists
Grown weepy over Jarrow photographs.
No comfort when the poor the state enlists
Parade before their fathers' cenotaphs.
No comfort when the strikers all go back
To see which twenty thousand get the sack.

Be with me when they cauterise the facts
Be with me to the bottom of the page,
Insisting on what history exacts.
Be memory, be conscience, will and rage,
And keep me cold and honest, cousin coat,
So if I lie, I'll know you're at my throat.

After Laforgue

In memory of Martin Bell

I have put a blockade on high-mindedness.
All night, through dawn and dead mid-morning,
Rain is playing rimshots on a bucket in the yard.
The weatherman tells me that the winter comes on
As if he'd invented it. Fuck him.

Fuck sunshine and airports and pleasure.
Wind is deadheading the lilacs inland.
You know what this means. I could sing.
The weekend sailors deal the cards and swear.
The Channel is closed. This is good.

In the sopping, padlocked, broad-leaved shade of money
Desperate lunches are cooking
In time for the afternoon furies and sudden,

Divorces of debt from the means of production.
Good also. These counties are closed.

Myself, I imagine the north in its drizzle,
Its vanished smoke, exploded chimneys: home
In bad weather to hills of long hospitals, home
To the regional problems of number, home
To sectarian strife in the precincts of Sheffield and Hartlepool,

Home from a world of late-liberal distraction
To rain and tenfoots clogged with leaves,
To the life's work of boredom and waiting,
The bus station's just-closing teabar,
The icy, unpromising platforms of regional termini,

Home to dead docks and the vandalized showhouse.
Home for Mischief Night and Hallowe'en, their little tales,
When the benches (the sodden repose of old bastards in
    dog-smelling overcoats)
Vanish, when council employees dragged from the pub
Will be dragging the lake in the park,

Watching their footprints fill up
And hating those whose bastard lives
Are bastard lived indoors. Home,
As Sunday extends towards winter, a shivery kiss
In a doorway, *Songs of Praise,* last orders. Home.

Rain, with an angel's patience, remind me.
This is not the world of Miss Selfridge and Sock Shop,
Disposable income and Lycra, illiterate hearsay
And just-scraping-in-after-Clearing to Business in Farnham.
This world is not Eastbourne. It has no opinions.

In this world it rains and the winter
Is always arriving rebirth of TB

And *The Sporting Green* sunk to the drainbed.
Here is the stuff that gets left in the gaps
Between houses—ambitious settees in black frogskin

And minibars missing their castors, the catalogues
Turning to mush, the unnameable objects
That used to be something with knobs on,
And now they live here, by the siding, the fishhouse,
The building whose function is no longer known.

It is Londesborough Street with the roof gone—
That smell as the wallpaper goes, as it rains
On the landing, on pot dogs and photos
And ancient assumptions of upright servility.
Nothing is dry. The pillow-tick shivers

And water comes up through the scullery tiles
And as steam from the grate. There are funerals
Backed up the street for a mile
As the gravediggers wrestle with pumps and the vicar
Attempts to hang on to his accent.

Rain, with an angel's patience, teach me
The lesson of where I came in once again,
With icy vestibules and rubber pillows,
The dick-nurse, the wet-smelling ash in the yard
And the bleary top deck like a chest ward.

Teach me the weather will always be worsening,
With the arctic fleet behind it—
The subject of talk in the shop, at the corner,
Or thought of when stepping out into the yard
To the sirens of factories and pilot-boats,

There like a promise, the minute at nightfall
When the rain turns to snow and is winter.

The Amateur God

Like sluggish electrons
The first gnats of April
Are cruising the visual field.
The kingfisher's moulting its plaster of Paris.
The cherub is moulting his head.
The goldfish stare up from cushions of weed,
Rehearsing blasé vowels at the sun.
The Peace rose,
Pruned to a barbed-wire paradox,
Stands with its label, as if on a platform
Awaiting the slow train of summer.
The gardener beats a new path out of cinder.
The brazier rolls its crimson eyes
Like Argus. There's nothing but detail
And leisure to name it, with one hand
To cool in the pond, and the other
Rubbing moss into my jeans
Wholeheartedly at thirty as at three.
The afternoon is permanent.
My father, my uncle, in suits of pale ash,
Are still sinking the black in the shade.
The voices of their politics
Are softer than the fountain's voice.
The afternoon is permanent.
The amateur god of this garden is me.

Alice Oswald was born in London in 1966 and now lives in Devon. With its mystical engagement with the natural world and almost heraldic tone, Oswald's work has naturally drawn comparisons with that of Ted Hughes. Oswald, though, is something like a modern metaphysical, and she often seems—against the grain of contemporary British practise—to wholly tell, and not show. Many of her shorter poems almost seem to attempt to eradicate the concrete altogether. Her voice is impossible to place in time, and she sounds the least contemporary of our poets, though—remarkably—not in the least archaic. The book-length poem *Dart*, a kind of mystical play for voices following the course of the River Dart in Devon, has proved to be exceptionally popular, though it will be interesting to see if Oswald can keep this readership when it discovers just how singularly uncompromising an artist she is.

FURTHER READING:
The Thing in the Gap-stone Stile (Oxford University Press, 1996), *Dart* (Faber & Faber, 2002)

April

The sheer grip and the push of it—growth gets
a footledge in the loosest stems, it takes
the litterings of weeds and clocks them round;
your eyeballs bud and alter and you can't
step twice in the same foot—I know a road,
the curve throws it one way and another;
somebody slipped the gears and bucketed slowly
into the hawthorns and his car took root
and in its bonnet now, amazing flowers
appear and fade and quiddify the month;
and us on bicycles—it was so fast
wheeling and turning we were lifted falling,
our blue-sky jackets filling up like vowels . . .
and now we float in the fair blow of springtime,
kingfishers, each astonishing the other

to be a feathered nerve, to take the crack
between the river's excess and the sun's.

Bike Ride on a Roman Road

This Roman road—eye's axis
over the earth's rococo curve—
is a road's road to ride in a dream.

I am bound to a star,
my own feet shoving me swiftly.

Everything turns but the North is the same.

Foot Foot, under the neck-high bracken
a little random man, with his head in a bad
controversy of midges,
flickers away singing Damn Damn

and the line he runs is serpentine,
everything happens at sixes and sevens,
the jump and the ditch and the crooked stile . . .

and my two eyes are floating in the fields,
my mouth is on a branch, my hair
is miles behind me making tributaries
and I have had my heart distracted out of me,
my skin is blowing slowly about without me

and now I have no hands and now I have no feet.

This is the road itself
riding a bone bicycle through my head.

Sea Sonnet

The sea is made of ponds—a cairn of rain.
It has an island flirting up and down
like a blue hat. A boat goes in between.

Is made of rills and springs—each waternode
a tiny subjectivity, the tide
coordinates their ends, the sea is made.

The sea crosses the sea, the sea has hooves;
the powers of rivers and the weir's curves
are moving in the wind-bent acts of waves.

And then the softer waters of the wells
and soakaways—hypostases of holes,
which swallow up and sink for seven miles;

and then the boat arriving on the island
and nothing but the sea-like sea beyond.

Wedding

From time to time our love is like a sail
and when the sail begins to alternate
from tack to tack, it's like a swallowtail
and when the swallow flies it's like a coat;
and if the coat is yours, it has a tear
like a wide mouth and when the mouth begins
to draw the wind, it's like a trumpeter
and when the trumpet blows, it blows like millions . . .
and this, my love, when millions come and go
beyond the need of us, is like a trick;

and when the trick begins, it's like a toe
tip-toeing on a rope, which is like luck;
and when the luck begins, it's like a wedding,
which is like love, which is like everything.

Prayer

Here I work in the hollow of God's hand
with Time bent round into my reach. I touch
the circle of the earth, I throw and catch
the sun and moon by turns into my mind.
I sense the length of it from end to end,
I sway me gently in my flesh and each
point of the process changes as I watch;
the flowers come, the rain follows the wind.

And all I ask is this—and you can see
how far the soul, when it goes under flesh,
is not a soul, is small and creaturish—
that every day the sun comes silently
to set my hands to work and that the moon
turns and returns to meet me when it's done.

℘ RUTH PADEL

Ruth Padel was born in London in 1947. Padel's favourite subject is love, the sensual, and their transformations. Padel is a classicist, and her poetry often seems pitched against the rigour of her other discipline—free-ranging, exhilaratingly associative, unbridled in its language and free flits of register. What impresses in Padel's work is the way she uses her unusual breadth of cultural reference to wholly unselfconscious ends; the high and the low achieve an oddly democratic balance in her work. Padel is also the author of several non-fiction titles on classical studies and music, and is a well-known critic and populiser of the art.

FURTHER READING:
Fusewire (Chatto & Windus, 1996) *Rembrandt Would Have Loved You* (Chatto & Windus, 1998)

Tinderbox

This is innocent. Teenage. Blossom
Without leaf. It's not a gun.
Not threatening anyone's conservatory,
Private school, or bank account.

Lies are being kept to a minimum
And lives are going on as they always have
And shall. We're only Noel Coward,
Lightest of light tenors, percolating

'Fate has sent me you'
Through the cherry-snow of Russell Square;
A hedgehog star of icicles lit
By the sun's last rays on the lip of a cliff.

The song will end,
The whole thing fall to pieces, when
We get to the forbidden mountain's heart.
It'll all be known. There'll be iron

With its cruel ideas. And maybe I'll stop
Saying the 'Our Father' in that narrow space
Between the bath and sweat-foxed
Mirror, hugging a towel

And thanking Someone, Anything,
For you. Morality. A trapdoor spider's
Inner web. A tinderbox. Where we are
Has no answers.

Skin

Remember how the screen
of your machine bruised
blue and milky as you touched it,
liquid under your fingers,

then faded as you touched
somewhere else: the whole
screen a going and coming
of bruises and fades?

Angel

No one sees me. Fathoms up
a nest of rays, all protein,
grey velvet triangles

six metres wing to wing,
a coat on them like a Weimerana,
ripples at the edges, slow,

the way the skite-tooth grass
trembled in lunar winds back home.
So no one knows

and if they read the impress
where my egg sacs
crumbled into bed, work done,

there's nothing they could do.
I listen to the humming
and I wait. Suppose they clawed

one ring from my antenna-bone
up through that tunnel of sea-cow
and acetta-swabs

changing sex halfway through life,
pink to meridian blue,
they'd re-do Linnaeus,

any story of black holes,
re-assign prizes
for the signature of matter,

but still they wouldn't
see what's coming.
How do I know all this?

Baby, where I come from,
we had pre-rusted pictoscopes
to tell us about aliens like you.

The Starling

They are talking of trepanning the Indian starling
because the starling thinks she is the Empress of Oslo
and besides, she is very lonely. The Kissagram boy,
off duty, brought her in from the westwoods
under the flyover, her tertiaries dipped in ink:
smaragdme plus a lavender-cum-royal blue.

She looked, then, a bedraggled poisonous orchid.
We bled her at the hip or wherever roughly
you might expect a hip in all that tininess.
She lies alone on puffed flannel and can't sleep.
I've slipped out, nights, against orders
to feed her cinnamon toast, read her The Golden Bough.

Her eye is cloudy, suspicious. She voids phlegm
and half-dreams of a childless woman
killed in a bar in backstreet Friedenstadt,
and that nobody, nobody mourned her
as the starling thinks she should be mourned.
Bedlam's Managing Director, the one man

who can save our starling, has evaded diagnosis.
He says it was a present from the King.
After the first incision, he kept his scalpel
under the raw lid of its Royal Society box
in a self-shaped baize hollow like the bed
of a chestnut in its shell. Or a sharp empty egg.

On the Line

Feel, you said. How does this feel?
Shy, if you must know,
to be asked.

But after, when you'd left
this all-gold absence
round me, in me, in even my cars,

I wondered. Sharp,
an axe on a bell.
Blast of the Trovatore chorus

when you open the oven door.
An extra-terrestrial
skiffle in the dish
at Jodrell Bank.

As if I'd never known red.
Hi-volt chillies
doing press-ups in a haybag of velvet.

An anaconda with hiccups.
Like the only thing. Like you.

∽ DON PATERSON

Don Paterson was born in Dundee in 1963. His books of poems have an astonishing formal and imaginative range that makes him difficult to pin down as a poet. He can dust off a sonnet and make it sound brand new, and he can work equally well with a variety of longer lyric and narrative modes. As has often been noted, he has an exquisite ear for language. He knows about history and he knows about love. His poems are irreverent, funny, erotic, sly, and always deeply intelligent.
—Charles Simic

FURTHER READING:
The White Lie: New and Selected Poems (Graywolf, 2001), *Landing Light* (Faber & Faber, 2003)

The White Lie

I have never opened a book in my life,
made love to a woman, picked up a knife,
taken a drink, caught the first train
or walked beyond the last house in the lane.

Nor could I put a name to my own face.
Everything we know to be the case
draws its signal colour off the sight
till what falls into that intellectual night

we tunnel into this view or another
falls as we have fallen. *Blessed Mother,*
when I stand between the sunlit and the sun
make me glass: and one night I looked down

to find the girl look up at me and through
me with such a radiant wonder, you
could not read it as a compliment
and so seek to return it; in the event

I let us both down, failing to display
more than a half-hearted opacity.
She turned her face from me, and the light stalled
between us like a sheet, a door, a wall.

But consider this: that when we leave the room,
the chair, the bookend or the picture-frame
we had frozen by desire or spent desire
is reconsumed in its estranging fire

such that, if we slipped back by a road
too long asleep to feel our human tread
we would not recognise a thing by name,
but think ourselves in Akhenaten's tomb.

Then, as things ourselves, we would have learnt
we are the source, not the conducting element.
Imagine your shadow burning off the page
as the dear world and the dead word disengage—

in our detachment we would surely offer
such offence to that Love that will suffer
no wholly isolated soul within
its sphere, it would blast straight through our skin

just as the day would flush out the rogue spark
it found still holding to its private dark.
But like our ever-present, all-wise god
incapable of movement or of thought,

no one at one with all the universe
can touch one thing; in such supreme divorce
what earthly use are we to our lost brother
if we must stay partly lost to find each other?

Only by this—this shrewd obliquity
of speech, the broken word and the white lie,
do we check ourselves, as we might halt the sun
one degree from the meridian

then wedge it by the thickness of the book
that everything might keep the blackedged look
of things, and that there might be time enough
to die in, dark to read by, distance to love.

St Brides: Sea-Mail

Now they have gone
we are sunk, believe me.
Their scentless oil, so volatile
it only took one stray breath on its skin
to set it up—it was our sole
export, our currency
and catholicon.

There was a gland
below each wing, a duct
four inches or so down the throat;
though it was tiresome milking them by hand
given the rumour of their infinite
supply, and the blunt fact
of our demand.

After the cull
we'd save the carcasses,
bind the feet and fan the wings,
sew their lips up, empty out their skulls
and carry them away to hang
in one of the drying-houses
twelve to a pole.

By Michaelmas,
they'd be so light and stiff
you could lift one up by its ankle
or snap the feathers from its back like glass.
Where their eyes had been were inkwells.
We took them to the cliffs
and made our choice.

Launching them,
the trick was to 'make
a little angel': ring- and fore-
fingers tucked away, pinkie and thumb
spread wide for balance, your
middle finger hooked
under the sternum.

Our sporting myths:
the windless, perfect day
McNicol threw beyond the stac;
how, ten years on, Macfarlane met his death
to a loopback. Whatever our luck,
by sunset, they'd fill the bay
like burnt moths.

The last morning
we shuffled out for parliament
their rock was empty, and the sky clear
of every wren and fulmar and whitewing.
The wind has been so weak all year
I post this more in testament
than hope or warning.

Imperial

Is it normal to get this wet? Baby, I'm frightened—
I covered her mouth with my own;
she lay in my arms till the storm-window brightened
and stood at our heads like a stone

After months of jaw jaw, determined that neither
win ground, or be handed the edge,
we gave ourselves up, one to the other
like prisoners over a bridge

and no trade was ever so fair or so tender;
so where was the flaw in the plan,
the night we lay down on the flag of surrender
and woke on the flag of Japan

ᴄᴨ PETER READING

Peter Reading was born in Liverpool in 1946. Reading is unusual in that while his work has been widely admired, he has no real acolytes (though his influence can be seen in the work of Alan Jenkins and Simon Armitage, amongst others). Few, anyway, would want to follow Reading where he has gone: 'unflinching' would imply a capacity to flinch in the first place, but it becomes quickly apparent that Reading's dead-eyed gaze is the only way he can find of approaching some almost unbearable human horrors. However his poems are, in the end, deeply humane affairs. His voice switches from that of a latterday Latin poet to an eerie ventrilo-quism of speech—the semiliterate, the thuggish—almost never represented on the page. Essentially an author of book-length poems, Reading is an impossible poet to represent fairly by extracts.

FURTHER READING:
Collected Poems 1 & 2 (Bloodaxe, 1995, 1996)

[from] Stet

Dirty sex violence of TV
    Should never be allowed
No wonder we can see
    The badly-behaved crowd!
Och! They will be punished
    On the Judgement Day,
Before the Lord is finished
    They will rue the day!
These do-gooder social workers
    Saying 'Let them go free'
Are all sinful shirkers
    Sent by Satan 'gainst you and me.
The way to stop these hooglums
    At football match or fight
Is string them up by thumbs
    Until they can tell Right
From Wrong, then ways of Jesus
    Will get into their heart

Which, at the present, freezes
　　And they know not where Love starts.

'Gie im a pint quick—diggin is grave wi is
prick e is, this bloke: seen im on Satdy night
　　parked in the Quarry, winders steamed-up,
　　　　flattened them oats o mine, randy fuckerrr'.

A bloke with whom I once worked at the mill,
one bait-time, in the Bait-Room, peeled the lid
back from his Tupper sandwich-box, produced
two off-white thick amorphous slabs of bread
wherefrom a pinkish greyish matter oozed.
He bit, considered, rolled blear red-veined eyes,
spat an envenomed mouthful on the floor,
hurled the offending bait-box to his feet
(Terpsichoreans might have found the way
he rain-danced it to smithereens beneath
steel-toe-capped boots inspired, original),
then opined 'Fucking stupid bloody cow!
Wait till I get the bitch; I'll give her *jam
over beef dripping*'! Next day he was off.
They did him (GBH?). She had to have
23 stitches—he was a big bloke.
One time, he'd been all day and half the night
hard on the piss (the Vaults and then the Club),
and on the way home stumbled against a white
new-painted door. Dismayed, he bought some meths
down at the late-night Chemist. In the house,
he dabbed his jacket liberally and then
fell asleep on the sofa. When his wife
came back from visiting her sister, she
found him in drunk repose reeking of meths,
the emptied bottle lying at his side.
She beat him with a heavy casserole-
dish (which had been a wedding present from

her mother, twenty-three long years before)
until the blood streamed. Some ententes rely
much on a reciprocity of malice.

Salopian

All day, the drone of a saw,
and resin across the pines
of dark Mortimer Forest.
With each completed sever
it fell by a whining octave.

By dusk, in the clearing they'd made,
all that remained was their dust,
the dottle from someone's pipe
and ranks of seasoning limbs
weeping congealing amber.

∞

The heat, the fragrance of hay,
the incontrovertible end
of summer, the country halt,
boarding the single-track train,
weeds prising the platform oblique
where they waved and waved and waved.

∞

Dewed cowslips, roses, the grave
under a yew in the garden
of lichened Pipe Aston church,
a dusty Visitors' Book . . .

We were once there: 17th
of June 1975.

ↄ **CHRISTOPHER REID**

Christopher Reid was born in Hong Kong in 1949 and now lives in London. Reid's tone almost approaches whimsy and litotes at times, but these methods are only employed to bluff the reader and prepare some thoroughly dark surprises. Reid writes exquisitely constructed poems of great wit and charm but is also—an aspect of his work too underpraised—capable of masterly dramatic monologues, in an impressive range of wholly convincing disguises. His flair for the arresting visual conceit had him briefly and mistakenly allied with the so-called 'Martian' school, but Reid's voice has long been one of the most singular and distinctive in English poetry.

FURTHER READING:
In the Echoey Tunnel (Faber & Faber, 1991), *Expanded Universes* (Faber & Faber, 1996)

A Whole School of Bourgeois Primitives

Our lawn in stripes, the cat's pyjamas,
rain on a sultry afternoon

and the drenching, mnemonic smell this brings us
surging out of the heart of the garden:

these are the sacraments and luxuries
we could not do without.

Welcome to our peaceable kingdom,
where baby lies down with the tiger-rug

and bumblebees roll over like puppies
inside foxglove-bells . . .

Here is a sofa, hung by chains
from a gaudy awning.

Two puddles take the sun
in ribbon-patterned canvas chairs.

Our television buzzes like a fancy tie,
before the picture appears—

and jockeys in art-deco caps and blouses
caress their anxious horses,

looking as smart as the jacks on playing-cards
and as clever as circus monkeys.

Douanier Rousseau had no need to travel
to paint the jungles of his paradise.

One of his tigers, frightened by a thunder-storm,
waves a tail like a loose dressing-gown cord:

It does not seem to match the coat at all,
but is ringed and might prove dangerous.

What the Uneducated Old Woman Told Me

That she was glad to sit down.
That her legs hurt in spite of the medicine.
That times were bad.
That her husband had died nearly thirty years before.
That the war had changed things.
That the new priest looked like a schoolboy and you could barely
     hear him in church.
That pigs were better company, generally speaking, than goats.
That no one could fool her.
That both her sons had married stupid women.
That her son-in-law drove a truck.

That he had once delivered something to the President's palace.
That his flat was on the seventh floor and that it made her dizzy to
    think of it.
That he brought her presents from the black market.
That an alarm clock was of no use to her.
That she could no longer walk to town and back.
That all her friends were dead.
That I should be careful about mushrooms.
That ghosts never came to a house where a sprig of rosemary had
    been hung.
That the cinema was a ridiculous invention.
That the modern dances were no good.
That her husband had had a beautiful singing voice, until drink
    ruined it.
That the war had changed things.
That she had seen on a map where the war had been fought.
That Hitler was definitely in Hell right now.
That children were cheekier than ever.
That it was going to be a cold winter, you could tell from the height
    of the birds' nests.
That even salt was expensive these days.
That she had had a long life and was not afraid of dying.
That times were very bad.

In the Echoey Tunnel

The little girl squealing
in the echoey tunnel,

scampering and squealing
just for the thrill of it,

spanking the pathway
with her own stampede of footfalls

and squealing, squealing
to make the brickwork tingle—

how fiercely she exults
in her brand-new discovery,

the gift of the tunnel
and its echoey gloom!

And then what a cheat,
to be dragged back to daylight!

Mermaids Explained

As he read the reports,
he saw at once
that all the mermaids
were dugongs or dolphins.

Their tresses were garlands
of sea vegetation,
or the billows they made
as they swam far off.

And what of the songs
that could lull and lure
impetuous mariners
to their downfall?

A tinnitus compounded
of wind and birds' cries
and something on the brain
too wicked to think about.

Fetish

I have in my possession
an angel's wingbone:
valueless, I gather,
without the certificate
of authentication
which can only be signed by a bishop.

I treasure it, however,
and almost religiously love
the sweet feel of its curve
between thumb and forefinger
deep in my jacket pocket,
the way I'm fondling it now.

Robin Robertson was born in 1955 in Aberdeen, Scotland. Already a highly influential editor, he published his first book relatively late in the day; his poems are highly elegant, darkly sexual, grave, and often bloody affairs. Robertson's exemplars are David Jones, Geoffrey Hill, and Michael Longley, though recent work has sounded a brighter note, especially in his nature poems, which seem to carry none of the despair he often seems to profess for his own species. At times Spanish in its shadows and French in its intellectual pessimism, Robertson's work in the end could be nothing but that of a Scot in the Dunbar lineage.

FURTHER READING:
A Painted Field (Picador, 1997); *Slow Air* (Picador, 2002)

Fall

    after Rilke

The leaves are falling, falling from trees
in dying gardens far above us; as if their slow
free-fall was the sky declining.

And tonight, this heavy earth is falling away
from all the other stars, drawing into silence.

We are all falling now. My hand, my heart,
stall and drift in darkness, see-sawing down.

And we still believe there is one who sifts and holds
the leaves, the lives, of all those softly falling.

Fugue for Phantoms

This is the heart's thorn: the red rinse of memory;
this is the call of the coronach—keening, keening

over the water, haunted water,
the pitched grey, gull-swept sea.

This is the net and trident, thrown and retrieved,
thrown again; this is the death we live through—
our own thoughts are the mesh that's cast,
that let in the past with a stabbing spear.

These are the strange stigmata, the memories that bleed;
these are the luminous ghosts: lures
on the barb that pulls the heart from darkness
and silence, to the surface of the sea.

Where they have risen, the sea-dead, bobbing in effigy:
skin gone to curd, and worn now like a fragile dress,
water behind the eyes like the insides of oyster shells;
their huge heads puckered, their faces pursed like lips.

I would commit it all to the deep;
I want never to remember anything of this.

Artichoke

The nubbed leaves
come away
in a tease of green, thinning
down to the membrane:
the quick, purpled,
beginnings of the male.

Then the slow hairs of the heart:
the choke that guards its trophy,
its vegetable goblet.

The meat of it lies, displayed,
up-ended, *al dente,*
the stub-root aching in its oil.

Wedding the Locksmith's Daughter

The slow-grained slide to embed the blade
of the key is a sheathing,
a gliding on graphite, pushing inside
to find the ribs of the lock.

Sunk home, the true key slots to its matrix;
geared, tight-fitting, they turn
together, shooting the spring-lock,
throwing the bolt. Dactyls, iambics—

the clinch of words—the hidden couplings
in the cased machine. A chime of sound
on sound: the way the sung note snibs on meaning

and holds. The lines engage and marry now,
their bells are keeping time;
the church doors close and open underground.

The Immoralist

In the sleeping ward, night-nurses
gather at my curtained bed,
looming like Rembrandts, drawing
their winged heads in around
the surgeon at my side.
The golden section lit by anglepoise:

the wrinkled fruit, some books,
my chest strapped like a girl's
to stem the leaking wound.

Scissoring the grey crêpe
released a clot dark as liver:
an African plum in its syrup
slid into my lap.
Jesus, I said, as the doctor called for swabs,
more light, the stitching trolley.
Without anaesthetics he worked quickly,
his pale hands deft
as a guitarist at the frets.
This is what they'd been waiting for:
one hand at the pliant flesh,
the other subduing it with suture
and a blurred knot.
Five minutes and it was over,
and he was smiling at the Gide
amongst the magazines and grapes:
Used to be just TB, this place, he said,
my blood on his cheek like a blush.
As the nurse drew back the curtain, she warned:
There will be pain.
Night flooded, streaming slowly into shape;
I heard the tinnitus of radio,
saw the humped figure under his lung of light,
the earphones' plastic stirrup on its hook,
his left hand in place on the white bandage
his right hand holding my book.

✑ ANNE ROUSE

Anne Rouse was born in 1954 and grew up in Virginia in the US. She has worked as a psychiatric nurse and has lived in London since the early '80s. Rouse is a poet of great formal deftness, with a fine gift for social satire and portraiture, and a comic's timing. Her formalism can sometimes disguise an experimental streak, however, and her poems are far more intricate constructions than their forms sometimes declare. These are socially and politically engaged poems of great wit and speed, informed by a keen literary intelligence and a talent for an almost forensically close observation of the species.

FURTHER READING:
Sunset Grill (Bloodaxe, 1993), *Timing* (Bloodaxe, 1997)

Testament

To my last technician,
I leave this flaming skeleton.

I like you better
than a doctor, or a hairdresser.

My leaving do's a blast, a whirl,
I'm a party girl,

Nude and ablaze like a tree,
one spectacular x-ray.

Look up from the gauges, be a voyeur,
a happy pyro-connoisseur,

But don't think to make free
with the calcine ash, the grit of me—

That's for a feeling hand,
or the wind.

Faith Healers

This could be the mind's antechamber:
Skylight, pre-war folding chairs, a stand of books,
The Psychic News, a hand-penned plea, DONATIONS:
Against each wall a lame hope waiting.

The ends of her sparse hair are a failed red,
She's stout and leads a shambling Alsatian.
'Through the veil' a limpid Jesus lifts his eyes
Above the nursery warmth, the funk of flowers.

The heaters of the clerestory
Burn among the eaves, vivid as lollies.
Patients play stone crusaders on the spindly beds.
The healers in their grocery macs

Press forehead, gut and thighs
Like John who spent his grace on strays
In a sirocco, a name for talisman.
They tend the dog, lay hands on anyone.

Memo to Auden

Wystan, you got off to a wrong start,
Being neither Catholic nor tubercular,
Nor a brash, alert provincial,
But you righted like a figure-skater
And traced your syntactical curlicues
Tight and fine, to make them news.

Out of the wry side of your mouth,
You dropped a flagrant quote or two.

With my dog-eared copy for credential,
I'd like to pick a minor bone with you.
Just pretend I'm fresh at public school
And try to keep your prefectorial cool.

Do you recall the tea shop on the Broad?
You'd agreed to sit there daily
At four o'clock and dawdle, bored,
A big cat, for an exhibition fee:
Available for metric consultation
To any undergrad with nerve, or vision.

Gaping there, I lost an opportunity.
In fact I spilled Darjeeling on your shoe
(Smart Oxford brogue), and nearly missed
Watching the Jo'burg tourist corner you.
He brought a semaphoric forearm down
To shake your hand, quite heedless of your frown,

Luminous with praise,
And bombast and italicised exclaiming.
Your work had meant a lot to him, especially
That famous poem I'd re-offend by naming—
No gavel-wielding judge has ever rapped it
So sharply as Your Honour did: 'I scrapped it'.

Now to the old gnawed bone, that poetry
Makes nothing happen, the report
Of someone flatly sidelined by a war,
Who feels embarrassed holding down the fort—
Unheroically and not from duty—
Of common intellect and beauty.

The worst horrors can't be quantified,
Can't be healed, denied, forgot,
But implicit in the name of peace

Are its varied fruits, that rot
Under a swastika; its vines that die
Tied to the paling of a lie.

What is the alternative to art?
Religion of guns, guns of religion.
You know all this. You said it well,
But you have a grumpy disposition,
So I'm repeating, like an awkward kid,
What you tell us, Dad, ain't what you did.

In the careful mornings of the art
Over tonic cuppas in the lay,
Not to speak of sweaty collaboration
With Isherwood, Kaltman, Britten, Stray,
You didn't do it for the bread alone:
Poets have to charm their bread from stone.

You didn't do it for the pick-up trade:
Most were arty foreigners, not rough.
You liked a wholesome share of fame,
But found the poet tag absurd enough
When talking with commercial sorts on trains.
Other professions call for verve and brains,

But you chose this one. Why?
Words are saucy, difficult but willing.
You could play boss and close the study door.
But there was another end, as thrilling
When the scholar's breath went sour:
Coaxing lines from beauty gave her power,

And this was the Holy: an act of love
To damn the bunker, damn the bomb,
And celebrate the individual life
Of myriad relations, from a room

Where the isolate voice is listened to
Through all its range, by such as you.

Let the victims, and their helpers,
And the guilty rest there for a time.
Let there be a commonality of good,
Gardens, architecture, rhyme,
That we betray by happenstance,
Forgiving airs to make us dance.

P.S. Myself I have too much to learn
Of voice and sense. You used this metre,
Don Juan too, but in our day
It's not exactly a world-beater.
Still, 'subtle' can mean convoluted
And for our little chat, it suited.

The Anaesthetist

This rubber pump in my hand sighs, pants, and wheezes
for you, my dear. Nighty-night, Ms Prynn.
Forbuoy approaches to wheel you in.
He is the theatre orderly. He is theatrical,

whipping off the dark green sheet like a tablecloth,
leaving you with nothing much to fall back on.
You are well under now, a gleaming cold matron.
Forbuoy is messing about with his pink slop.

The surgeon pulls latex over his finger joints;
the nurse displays her swift knives and forks.
Forbuoy and his shadow start to snigger, the oiks,
in the holy second of waiting.

The present, powerful, naked Ms Prynn
glows and is bold, illumined further
by the big lamp lowered like a flying saucer
as it hovers, stops.

Then round that star-lit table we are all drawn in.
You are turned and covered; your back basted pink.
I touch your wrist, while you stumble in your Hades walk,
Ms Prynn, at the first, sharp rocks.

ও JO SHAPCOTT

Jo Shapcott was born in London in 1953. Shapcott often seems to attempt nothing less than a wholly conscious surrealism, where so much is both strange and utterly convincing. Her work asserts the primacy of the vision and the pure imaginative flight, albeit one directed by a fierce intellectual rigor. Unsurprisingly, she has been increasingly drawn to the work of the Rilke and has produced a book, *Tender Taxes*, based on Rilke's French poems; the book is neither version nor imitation but enters into strange cross-gendered dialogue with the original poems that point towards a wholly new way of approaching the translated text, and confirms her reputation as one of the most original voices in the language.

FURTHER READING:
Her Book: Poems 1988–1998 (Faber & Faber, 1999), *Tender Taxes* (Faber & Faber, 2001)

Muse

When I kiss you in all the folding places
of your body, you make that noise like a dog
dreaming, dreaming of the long run he makes
in answer to some jolt to his hormones,
running across landfills, running, running
by tips and shorelines from the scent of too much,
but still going with head up and snout
in the air because he loves it all
and has to get away. I have to kiss deeper
and more slowly—your neck, your inner arm,
the neat creases under your toes, the shadow
behind your knee, the white angles of your groin—
until you fall quiet because only then
can I get the damned words to come into my mouth.

My Life Asleep

Everything is loud: the rasp of bed-sheets,
clamour of hair-tangles, clink of teeth.
Small sweat takes up residence in each crease
of the body, but breathing's even, herself warm,
room safe as a London room can be.
The tube rumbles only metres underneath
and planes for Heathrow circle on the roof.
You'll find the body and all the air it exhales
smellier than by day; she's kinder, more supple.
Bend close to catch the delicacies of sleep,
to hear skin tick, to taste the mandragora
of night sweat. Lean forward and put a finger
on the spot you think the dream is.

Motherland

after Tsvetaèva

Language is impossible
in a country like this. Even
the dictionary laughs when I look up
'England', 'Motherland', 'Home.'

It insists on falling open instead
three times out of the nine I try it
at the word Distance. *Degree
of remoteness, interval of space.*

Distance: the word is ingrained like pain.
So much for England and so much
for my future to walk into the horizon
carrying distance in a broken suitcase.

The dictionary is the only one
who talks to me now. Says, laughing,
'Come back HOME!' but takes me
further and further away into the cold stars.

I am blue, bluer than water
I am nothing, while all I do
is waste syllables this way.

England. It hurts my lips to shape
the word. This country makes me say
too many things I can't say. Home
of me, myself, my motherland.

The Mad Cow in Love

I want to be an angel and really think
I'm getting there with this mind of mine,
shrinking every day towards the cleanness,
the size of a baby animal's brain.
Trouble is, I want you to be an angel too
—and want that more if anything. It's one
of those demands I can't raise just like that,
evenings, when we're reading our different newspapers
you scanning your pages and me mine for an item
to start speech, make mouths smile, knees touch—something
in all that murder and mayhem to launch love.
You tell me you're looking for news of the self.
Do you want to be an angel? I know
the answer already and it's rough medicine.
But think of all the kinds there are, as many
as the different degrees of reaching
for the good. You might get away without
searching for the soul at all in those places,

today at least, you'd rather not get to know.
And angels do a variety of jobs:
the post of perpetual adoration might suit,
or divine messenger but I fancy for you
the government of the stars and all the elements.
I know you well enough to choose, after all this time
as foreign correspondent on the track of who you are,
looking for leads: your last screw, the food
you threw away, your strategic approaches
for living through the next hour. I don't mean it,
though, any of it. I want you earthly,
including all the global terrors and harms
which might come when we fall backwards
into the world of horn and hoof.

Phrase Book

I'm standing here inside my skin,
which will do for a Human Remains Pouch
for the moment. Look down there (up here).
Quickly. Slowly. This is my own front room

where I'm lost in the action, live from a war,
on screen. I am an Englishwoman, I don't understand you.
What's the matter? You are right. You are wrong.
Things are going well (badly). Am I disturbing you?

TV is showing bliss as taught to pilots:
Blend, Low silhouette, Irregular shape, Small,
Secluded. (Please write it down. Please speak slowly.)
Bliss is how it was in this very room

when I raised my body to his mouth,
when he even balanced me in the air,

or at least I thought so and yes the pilots say
yes they have caught it through the Side-Looking

Airborne Radar, and through the J-Stars.
I am expecting a gentleman (a young gentleman,
two gentlemen, some gentlemen). Please send him
(them) up at once. This is really beautiful.

Yes they have seen us, the pilots, in the Kill Box
on their screens, and played the routine for
getting us Stealthed, that is, Cleansed, to you and me,
Taken Out. They know how to move into a single room

like that, to send in with Pinpoint Accuracy, a hundred Harms.
I have two cases and a cardboard box. There is another
bag there. I cannot open my case—look out,
the lock is broken. Have I done enough?

Bliss, the pilots say, is for evasion
and escape. What's love in all this debris?
Just one person pounding another into dust,
into dust. I do not know the word for it yet.

Where is the British Consulate? Please explain.
What does it mean? What must I do? Where
can I find? What have I done? I have done
nothing. Let me pass please. I am an Englishwoman.

Index of Authors and Titles

Index of First Lines

This rubber pump in my hand sighs, pants, and wheezes / 178
To my last technician, / 174
To Rowntrees one morning / 57
We're out in my father's boat and he's fishing. / 78
What is it made of? Guilt. Blame. Sometimes, / 114
What was I doing here, haunting the dead? / 110
What was it you said again there by the river / 116
When I kiss you in all the folding places / 180
When I learned that my parents were returning / 99
When proof of Einsten's Glaswegian birth / 35
Who grows old in fifty pages of Plutarch: / 102
Wystan, you got off to a wrong start, / 175
Yes, love, that's why the warning light comes on. Don't / 8
You are my secret coat. You're never dry. / 143
You are the plainest moon. Forget all others: / 64
You sleep little and light / 36
Your shaved head on my thigh / 83

DON PATERSON was born in Dundee in 1963. He works as a writer and musician, teaches at the University of St Andrews, and is Poetry Editor for Picador Books. He has published four collections of verse, the most recent of which is *Landing Light* (2003), winner of the Whitbread Award. His selected poems are published by Graywolf as *The White Lie* (2001). He has won a number of literary awards, including the T. S. Eliot Prize, a Forward Prize, and the Geoffrey Faber Memorial Award. Paterson lives in Kirriemuir, Scotland.

CHARLES SIMIC is a poet, essayist, and translator. He has published sixteen collections of his own poetry, five books of essays, a memoir, and numerous books of translations, for which he has received many literary awards, including the PEN Translation Award. His collection of prose poems, *The World Doesn't End*, won the 1990 Pulitzer Prize. *The Voice at 3:00 A.M.*, his selected and new poems, was a finalist for the National Book Award. Simic teaches American literature and creative writing at the University of New Hampshire.

This book has been typeset using Trump Mediäval, a typeface designed by Georg Trump and first issued in 1954 by the Weber Foundry, Stuttgart, Germany. Book design by Wendy Holdman. Composition at Stanton Publication Services, Inc., St. Paul, Minnesota. Manufactured by Friesens on acid-free paper.